THE ART OF
INTERACTIO

University College for the Creative
at Canterbury, Epsom, Farn'

Epsom, Ash'   ‾
Return or

2
3

THE ART OF EXPERIMENTAL
INTERACTION DESIGN

This book is a survey of creative work from 30 studios and individuals from around the world. The contributors have different backgrounds and work in different circumstances – some in commercial design studios, others as fine artists or gallerists or as teachers, others again as students. What these diverse contributors have in common is that they all work within the relatively new field of interaction design, and that their work is in some way experimental, that they have each, to a greater or lesser degree, found a new way of using interactive media, and thereby extended the language of interactivity.

This might sound like a big claim on behalf of a little book and its 30 contributors, but it's not as overstated as it seems. Interaction design is an emerging practice, and the language of interactivity is still forming. In this context, adopting an experimental approach to the design process is not so much an indulgence as a necessity. There is an enormous design space out there and much of it has not been explored yet. This became clear to me in a direct way during the time I spent in the antirom studio in London, from the mid to late 1990s. There was no body of previous work to draw on, no books or manuals from which we could learn while, for example, creating an interactive shop window, or putting together an interactive installation in a museum or gallery. At a very basic level we had to work it out for ourselves, and that meant experimenting with the medium and the audience. The process was a combination of inventing and discovering – inventing in the sense of coming up with a new way of communicating with the medium, discovering in the sense that this would then be tested with an audience and either adopted, modified or discarded, depending on the results. Although others may have worked on similar problems and have come up with similar solu-

tions, we didn't know it at the time and so for us the process was one of real discovery and real invention. These are still the conditions in which much interaction design takes place today.

One of the reasons for this lies in the difference of interactivity with respect to other more established modes of communication which have longer histories and more clearly defined languages – cinema, print or broadcast media for example. These involve a linear presentation with a clearly defined separation between the sender of the message – the author – and the receiver of the message – the audience. The form of the message is broadly that of the proposition or statement – the author tells the audience something about the world, more often than not within a narrative structure. Interactive media by contrast involves a blurring of the line between author and audience in which the audience, to a certain extent, participates in the creation of the message itself. Indeed, many interactive pieces can hardly be said to contain a message at all, at least not in the form of a proposition or statement. Rather they involve the audience within a situation which they are invited to explore, or they offer the audience a game or toy with which they are invited to play. The meaning of the experience becomes the experience itself. So with a piece like *Power Flower* created by Antenna for Bloomingdales in New York, in which the line of neon flowers in the store window light up as people pass by on the street outside, the meaning lies in the playfulness of the experience, a primary sense of charm and delight in the very responsiveness of the artefact, rather than in any more elaborate statement about flowers, or light, or walking. A good interactive design may be weak on reference but full of something else, best described as emotional.

In *Trigger Happy, (The Inner Life of Videogames)*, Steve Poole quotes Plato's definition of play: 'That which has neither utility nor truth nor likeness, nor yet, in its effects is harmful, can best be judged by the criterion of the charm which is in it, and by the pleasure it affords. Such pleasure, entailing as it does no appreciable good or ill, is play'.

The key words here are 'charm' and 'play'. They are as important to understanding interaction design as they are to videogame design, and they point to a strong connection between these disparate practices. Indeed videogames might properly be viewed as part of interaction design in the broadest sense of the term, even if the investment in research and development within the global gaming industry is of a wholly different order. I have not included commercial videogames in this book, but their influence can be felt across the work of many of the contributors, from Delaware with their *Walk on the Hill* to Tomato's *Wisp* for the PS2, Grahame Weinbren's experiments in interactive narrative or Ryota Kawukubo's *Loopscape*. All, like the best videogames, involve the audience within a playful situation, all impart a sense of charm which has to be experienced to be fully appreciated, none of them are overly concerned with 'truth', at least not in the sense that might be recognized by a Greek philosopher. These qualities are also to be found in the masterpieces of video gaming, in Zelda or Super Mario Bros, in Asteroids or Rez.

If Plato is the Granddaddy of writers on play, then Huizinga has to be the stern Father. In Homo Ludens, the least playful book on play imaginable, Huizinga links games and music through their shared connection with the verb 'to play'. Across different language groups around the world, the word 'play' means both 'to play a game' and 'to play a musical instrument'. Huizinga suggests that this demonstrates a strong affinity between these activities, and that playing an instrument, is equivalent, in a formal sense at least, to playing a game. The idea of interactive music based on new devices that embody a sense of playfulness which is musical and toy-like and charming, is one that has pre-occupied interaction designers for some years, and seems likely to continue to do so. The piano was, at the time of its invention nearly 200 years ago, an extraordinary feat of design and high tech engineering that changed the way music was composed, performed and listened to. The sound toys – or new instruments – of today are having a similar effect in blurring the line between musician and non-musician and allowing more people to cross over from listening to performing.

Romandson's *Composition Station* at the Wellcome Wing in the Science Museum, London, is a high tech Gamelan – a four player installation which explores what happens when you combine a 3 part rhythm with one with 4 parts, or 17 with 11, or any other combination of numbers. *TapTap* from the RCA is an extraordinarily effective modular sound box that reproduces whatever simple percussive rhythm is applied to its surface, including the beat from another *TapTap*. As with the *Composition Station*, the complex permutations which can ensue from such a simple premise are endless. *Shaker*, also from the RCA, is a beaker which the user can fill with sound, and then trigger and transform by spinning, tilting and shaking. Ryota Kuwakubo and Sony's *Blockjam* is a sequencer which the user plugs together like so many Lego bricks into a physical model which is also a musical composition. In *Composing* by ART+COM at the Jewish Museum in Berlin, a Daniel Libeskind alphabet is connected to a sound sequencer to create both a piece of music and a floor plan, which, if the music is good, can be developed into a full architectural model.

If interaction design and the design of musical instruments are connected at some deep level, *Composing* points to another affinity, that between interaction design and architecture. Both offer a space within which to act and both sketch a potential for a meaning – a meaning moreover which can never be fully realised by the designer alone, but only in partnership with the user. The combination of interactive media and architecture can create what Lev Manovich has called 'augmented space', a real space overlaid with another, virtual layer of responsiveness. Ron Arad's collaboration with Tomato Interactive on *Delight in Dedark* – a real curtain with a virtual curtain projected onto it – is a good example of this. Klein Dytham Architecture's work with Toshio Iwai – *Interactive Communication Experience* – for Bloomberg in Tokyo is another. There is the *Interactive Shop Window* for Levi Strauss by Antirom, Ideo's *Message Wall* for 02 and Ars Electronica Futurelab's reactive building for SAP in Berlin. What all of these partnerships demonstrate is the extraordinary potential for crossover between interactivity and architectural or interior design, and the complementary relationship which these disciplines can enter into.

They're also all more or less commercial projects. In my original call for submissions for this book I made it clear that I positively welcomed proposals from commercial designers as well as artists – the fine art world has no monopoly on creativity, especially not creativity which aspires to being both experimental and interactive. On the contrary, much of the most interesting work seems to take place outside the art world, or at least on its margins. Maybe no surprises here given the conservative and herd-like nature of the fine art crowd. Maybe the technical skills which interactive artists tend to have are considered to be a little, well, geeky, not really the thing. Nonetheless it would be nice to see a major artist like Golan Levin get a little more recognition outside of specialist interactive or electronic arts circles. Landesign's Peter Higgens in an interview with IDonline is to the point. When asked what he found most inspiring in 2002, Higgens replied:

"The work of Ars Electronica artist-in-residence Golan Levin, and Raphael Lozano Hemmer's *Body Movies* touring show." And most disappointing? "The failure of Tate Modern to include such work."

A book like this can only be a partial survey of an emerging field of practice. I have included those projects I know about, some of which I was directly involved in producing through my involvement in antirom, Romandson or Fabrica. I apologise to those artists and designers who have done great work and who I haven't included, either through ignorance or lack of time or space. Among these, I particularly regret the absence of Ron Arad's interactive floor, another of his works done in collaboration with Tomato, in which the user can physically remodel the floor of a space via hydraulic rams, and Scott Snibbe's extraordinary *Deep Walls*. I also regret the lack of *Processing* by Casey Reas et al – an ambitious piece of work which is doing so much to bring powerful tools and a sense of creative community to interactive artists and designers around the world. Finally I must mention both Studio Azzurro, who explore the poetics of situation with their powerful video installations, and James Clar's *3D Display Cube* – a hand soldered three dimensional lattice of steel wire and glass bulbs which is almost as beautiful dark as when animated by light.

One thing has become clear to me during the making of this book. There is a tremendous surge of creative work in interactive art and design as more and more people get excited about new tools, and develop new ideas for using them. It's not the first time designers and artists have responded enthusiastically to new technological opportunities. However, with programmed, non-linear and interactive media, a whole set of assumptions about how communication works, at a formal level, have to be reexamined. It's our lack of understanding about this aspect of the medium – how it works as a language – that makes it all so breathlessly exciting. Don't believe those who tell you interaction design is a buzz phrase past its sell-by-date. We've only just begun to play.

Andy Cameron, Fabrica

ANTENNA

Masamichi Udagawa and Sigi Moeslinger formed Antenna in 1997. Here they explain why.

"When a new technology (in an abstract sense) is inserted into an existing socio-cultural fabric, it has to negotiate how this entry can be made. In this process, technology becomes tangible and has a new meaning assigned to it. We are quite keen to be involved in projects that embody this process. Our approach to interactivity is strongly informed by our background in product design. Using a product or moving through an environment is inherently a process of reciprocal actions. We see the application of digital interactive technology as an extension of this reciprocal nature of products and environments. So we apply the same thinking. We design for and around the users. We try to predict their behaviour and design to guide them through a series of prescribed actions, which trigger desired events. When we talk about users in this context, we need to point out that there is no such thing as a 'practical' use in our interactive installations – their purpose is to delight, to evoke new sensations, to change our perception of a particular environment."

Power Flower,
Bloomingdale's, New York, January 2002.
"The interactive light-and-sound installation features a series of neon flowers that 'bloom' when passers-by trigger motion sensors. As people continue to move past the store's Lexington Avenue windows, the first flowers triggered will quickly fade out, while new ones brighten up, leaving a wave-like trail behind every passer-by. As more people pass, the illuminated flowers create a brilliant display of light and sound.
"New York is a city of perpetual animation. The installation visualises the energy that radiates from the people of New York in a poetic manner."

Blowing Gently,
Frederieke Taylor Gallery, New York, 2002.
"The installation is a reflection on ephemerality. The visitor is faced with a minimalistic set-up featuring a large, monolithic object from which two polished aluminum rings curiously protrude. The aluminum rings evoke the memory of a nostalgic childhood trinket, the soap-bubble toy, thus hinting at the mode of interaction: the subtle action of blowing. Visitors become an integral part of the installation, as it is their breathing that unfolds a chain of events.

"By blowing at different lengths and intensities, visitors create and inflate male and female creatures, which subsequently seem to float off into space. Each creature has an individual behaviour that causes different reactions when they collide with one another. Eventually all creatures fade away, disappear into a void or simply pop.
"A smaller piece, *Day Six,* also activated by the visitor's breath, plays on the creation myth. Visitors are invited to breathe various randomly selected qualities into their own image via a pair of abstracted nostrils in front of a mirror. When blowing, one can watch oneself exhaling and inhaling a swarm of images representing qualities such as youth or beauty, which appear floating in the mirror."

Cherry Blossom,
Cooper-Hewitt National Design Museum April 2003.
"*Cherry Blossom* is situated in the centre of the Grand Staircase of the museum. The installation is an intervention in an existing path, thereby turning everyone who is walking up or down the stairs into a performer. A two-storey semi-cylinder in the middle of the staircase serves as a projection screen. When someone walks on the stairs, each step triggers the projection of a ring of swirling cherry blossoms, relative to that step, accompanied by a sound effect.
"The more people there are on the staircase, the more blossoms are triggered, resulting in an opulent display of shades of pink illuminating the space. When no-one is on the staircase, the projection turns into falling snow, suggesting that it is people's movement that is a source of warmth and beauty."

Firefly,
Brooklyn Bridge Anchorage, New York, June 2001.
"*Firefly* augments the Anchorage with a fictional presence. Skeletal self-illuminated objects, intended to be perceived as light rather than material, are scattered throughout the Anchorage. These furniture-like objects are hinting at the existence of an imaginary domestic space super-imposed on the Anchorage.
"By using a Palm OS device, the viewer can be beamed 'reactive animations' that complement the particular object, e.g., a skeletal faucet with rippling water or a cage with touch-sensitive fireflies. The trail of objects leads to a grassy slope for viewer relaxation and contemplation of our physical and immaterial world."

Cherry Blossom

Power Flower

POWER FLOW
MASAMICHI UDAGAWA AND SIGI
ANTENNA DESIGN

Blowing Gently

Blowing Gently

Firefly

Firefly

ANTIROM

The Antirom collective was formed in 1994 by a group of Londoners as a protest against "ill-conceived point-and-click 3D interfaces" grafted onto re-purposed old content-video, text, images, audio and so on – and repackaged as multimedia. The members of Antirom felt they could do better than this multimediocrity, or at least no worse.

The idea was to explore interactivity and try to understand what made an interactive experience engaging – an apparently simple question, but one that proved difficult to resolve. Inspired by Gerald Van Der Kaap's *BlindRom*, Antirom's eponymous first CD-ROM was a collection of small interactive pieces that were playful, fun, often silly and that usually explored only one interactive idea at a time.

The group developed hundreds of small interactive pieces, or so-called "toys". Each toy was highly playful, without the complexity or competitiveness of a game, and in which the pleasure comes from the playing, not the winning – a very English approach.

Crucially, many of these toys were produced rapidly, with prototypes passed around the studio and each member of Antirom adding or changing their version. This iterative design process produced a plethora of versions, many of which were blind alleys, but some of which survived to evolve into finished versions.

The original *Antirom* CD-ROM was self-published and funded by a grant from the Arts Council of Great Britain. Some 1,000 CDs were pressed and given away. Tomato contributed graphically to the *Antirom* CD-ROM and then underground trance dance trio, Underworld, let them use some of their music.

Long before Nike and Sony created their online experimental galleries, *Nikelab* and *The Third Place*, Levi Strauss understood the resonance that interactive media had with its customers. In 1995, Levi's approached Antirom to re-design its interactive in-store kiosk.

The *Levi Strauss in-store kiosk* series offered customers a range of interactive toys – some based on the product, some not. The first version had a *People* toy with hundreds of vox pop interviews shot in Soho, which the user could re-edit in real time by clicking on the video.

Later, the *Levi Strauss kiosk* became host to a range of interactive sound-mixing toys, VJ engines, interactive cable TV spoofs, 3D sequencers and webcam toys. As ISDN began to roll out, Antirom created a network webcam game between Levi's stores in London and Berlin, loosely based on the Neoprint photo-sticker craze.

Keen to get away from the basic computer interfaces of mouse and keyboard, Antirom started to experiment with external sensors to trigger elements on screen. This led to the creation of an interactive shop window for Levi's. Using touch sensors that could be activated through glass and a large plasma screen in the shop window, Antirom developed a selection of interactive toys that would work with a grid of nine sensors stuck to the window. These toys included sound mixers and simple drum machines that foreshadowed the popular *Namco Drum Mania* and *Dance Dance Revolution* arcade games.

The simplicity of the interactive toys, combined with an interface that was triggered by such simple actions as slapping the window, was a popular hit. Passers-by would stop and play with the interactive window whether the store was open or not. The plate glass windows were bulletproof so that even the most vigorous late-night attempts at playing with the toys were safe.

Antirom disbanded as a commercial entity in 1999 and its members have gone on to be part of companies such as Tomato, Romandson, The Big Space, PokeLondon, Studio Three, Animal Logic and institutions such as the University of Westminster (where many of them studied) and the Royal College of Art in London, The University of New South Wales in Australia, Fabrica in Italy and the Kunsthochschule in Kassel, Germany.

Levi's interactive window sensor

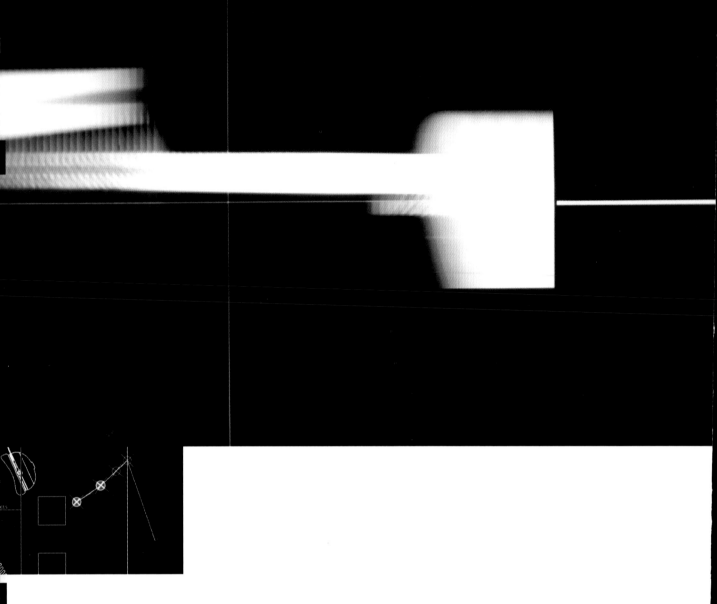

Tomato CD-rom
Levi's retail kiosk

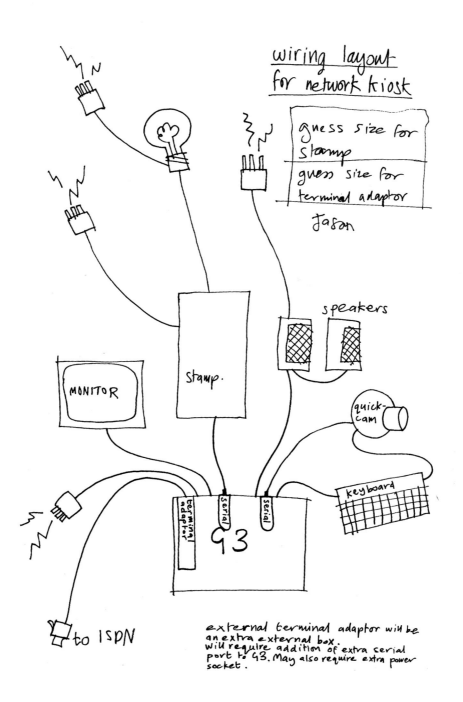

wiring layout
for network kiosk

guess size for
stamp
guess size for
terminal adaptor

Jason

speakers

quick-
cam

keyboard

MONITOR

stamp.

terminal
adaptor

serial

serial

G3

to ISDN

external terminal adaptor will be
an extra external box.
Will require addition of extra serial
port to G3. May also require extra power
socket.

Wiring sketch for Levi's networked
camera kiosk

ARS ELECTRONIC FUTURELAB

Integrated within the Ars Electronica network, this in-house R&D lab works at the nexus of art, technology and business.

The Hidden World of Voice and Noise,
SAP Headquarters, Berlin
"The Ars Electronica Futurelab worked with Golan Levin and Zach Lieberman to turn the SAP Headquarters in Berlin into a reactive building. Levin and Lieberman developed software that visualises sound in real time, based on their previous body of work in this field. The main focus of the project was to create a sense of life within the building, even when it was empty. To this end, a whole range of input devices was installed in order to allow the immediate environment to animate the building. Microphones were placed outside the building so that passers-by could interact with the visual displays inside by making a noise out in the street. At night, large-format projection screens alllowed spectators on the outside to see the path of the sound images throughout the entire building. Cameras were used to track the motion of people walking through the building, creating waves and ripples on display screens. Heartbeat sensors installed next to the the entrance invited visitors to place their hands on a metal surface. The sensors picked up the human pulse. Lights and projections in the lobby, and levels immediately above the lobby, throbbed in rhythm with the pulse of the user.
"An interactive bar consisted of tables on which customers could put their drinks. They were able to manipulate the dynamic objects projected onto the table's surface with their fingers and pass them between tables. When a drinker left a glass of beer on the table, the objects circled around it, as if protecting it."

The Hidden World of Noise and Voice

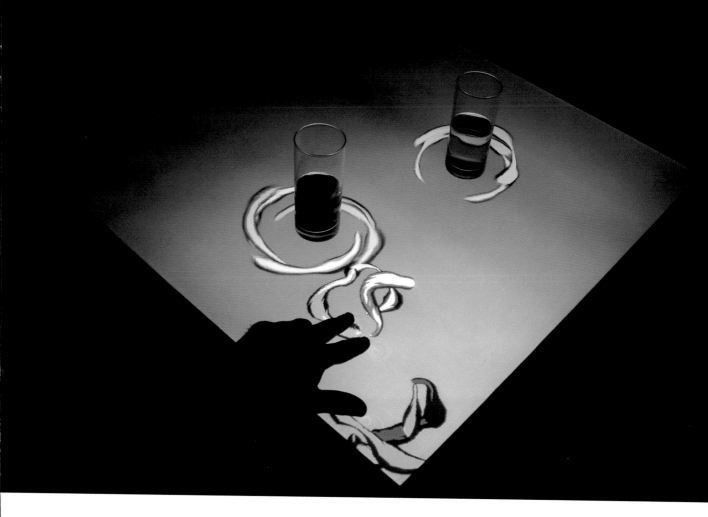

ART+COM

Founded way back in 1988, ART+COM reckons it is probably just about the oldest New Media design group around. Its original premise was to explore the notion that the computer is a medium, not just a tool, and the plan was to do research into digital communication and media art. In the early '90s, however, when it began to be offered large-scale industrial and commercial projects, it became a "proper" company. One of ART+COM's early projects was *Iconoclast*, a system for displaying artworks that tracked the viewer's eye movements and erased whichever part of the image was being looked at. Joachim Sauter, a director and one of the firm's founders, describes his background thus: "I studied visual communication and film in the late '70s and I didn't set eyes on my first Macintosh computer until 1984. I got really interested in it and taught myself programming – first Basic, then Lingo, then Java and then C++. I started ART+COM in 1988". "I don't program anymore," he said. "It's more efficient to let a proper programmer do it for me now." These days, Joachim is increasingly aware that more and more designers can also code and he believes that the crossover between computing and design – computational design – will become ever more important in the future. "The '90s were a time when there was a lot of technical innovation," he said. "Now the important thing is to prove the value of these new technologies, and this new medium, by using them to create high-quality communication. It's all about real projects now."

The Wall

"*The Wall* is part of a showroom for a company that sells street furniture – street lamps, public toilets, bus stops and so on. The idea was to create a powerful interactive installation, with a strong linear dramaturgy, which can be used to make a commercial presentation to a small number of clients. The presenter can interact with *The Wall* to control the depth of information displayed, literally and figuratively. The image of a virtual toilet can be scanned, sliced and all of its insides displayed. As *The Wall* moves backwards and forwards, different layers of information are highlighted. The installation forges a direct connection between the virtual and the real."

Floating Numbers

"*Floating Numbers* is a design installation commissioned by the Jewish Museum in Berlin that seeks to help visitors explore and understand 'the meaning of numbers'. There are a lot of numbers in the world, and a very large number of different meanings have been attached to them – religious, historical, philosophical and so forth. The challenge for ART+COM was how to help the visitor come to terms, in a playful way, with such a disconcertingly large amount of information. So it created a massive table display – 9 x 2 metres – over which flows a stream of digits. As individual numbers float up to the surface of the stream, the visitor can touch them and find out more about their meanings."

Composing

"The second work commissioned by the Jewish Museum of Berlin is an art piece based on an alphabet of pictograms created by the museum's architect, Daniel Liebeskind. He developed different alphabets for different sections of the museum. In *Composing*, the visitor can use one of these alphabets to create both a piece of music based on the 12-tone composition method – and the floor plan of an imaginary building. If the user likes the music, then he or she can activate it further and the floor plan is rendered as a 3D model."

The Wall

Alles aus einer Hand | Für Städte. Für Menschen.
Single Source Solution | For Cities. For People.

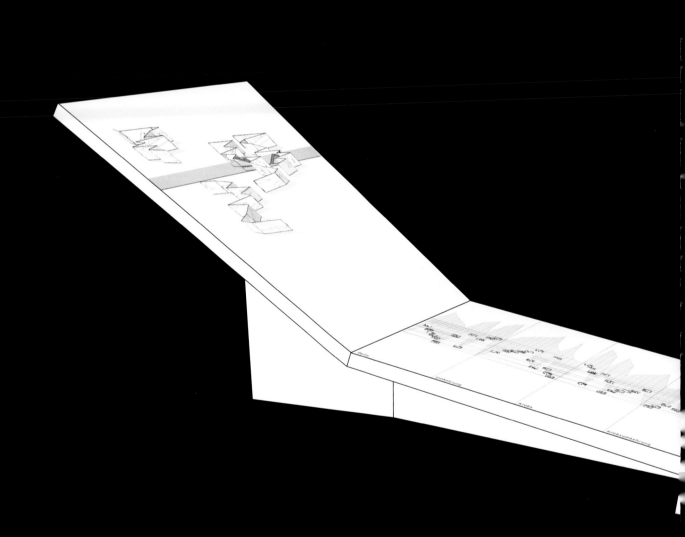

Composing

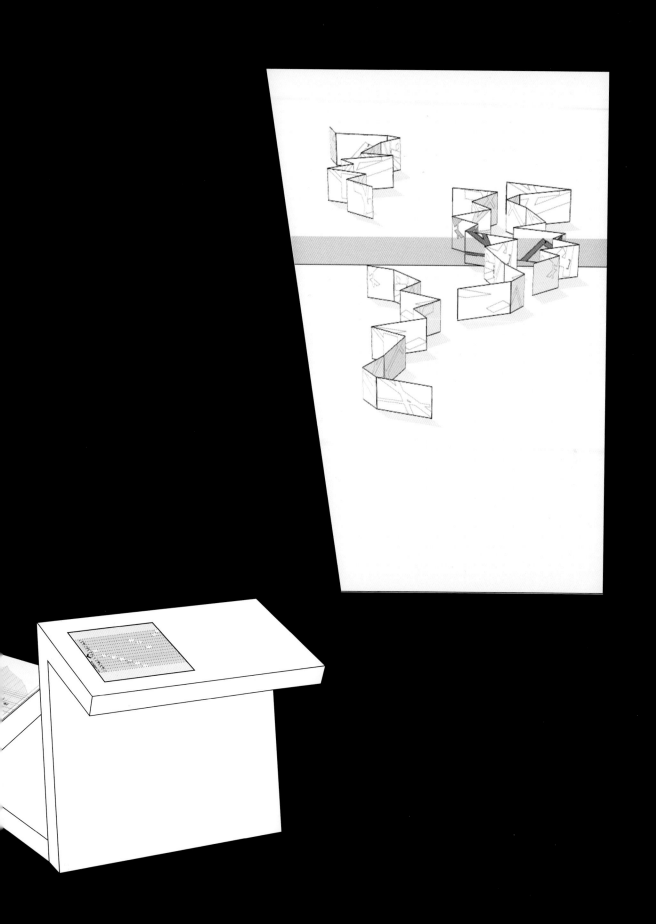

BIGSPACE

Bigspace is a Milan based design consultancy that in their own words, "use the tools of new media – film production, sound, graphics, and interactive design – to perfect the art of illusion in everyday life, beyond language and logic, drawing the line between art and commercial viability and creating worlds of magic."

Il Pozzo / The Well – Ta Matete, Rome
"A round stone structure in the shape of an ancient Roman well standing a meter high and two meters in diameter. A projector is positioned underneath the structure on the floor below, rear-projecting onto an etched glass surface. The outer edge of the surface is lined with electro-magnetic sensors that react to any physical contact to the surface. A pulsing light emits from underneath the structure. Speakers integrated into the floor around the structure provide ambient sound and vibration.

"An endless source of whirling letters appear from the depths of the well and float away from the centre of the screen in all directions. Randomly, letters come together to form words in different languages at the outer edges of the surface. When a word is formed the nearest user simply touches the surface. Once a word is touched the letters descend to the bottom of the well and an animation sequence of a work of art surfaces, enabling all users around the well to enjoy the content."

Fiat Lancia – Printemps
"A carousel of three brand animations react to the ambient sound levels in the space. As the voices in the space become louder, the animations become more active. A digital finger painting application offers users the opportunity to design their own custom version of the Lancia Ypsilon. People choose between a palette of 16 different textures to paint their car. After completing their design, users may print their creation and take it home."

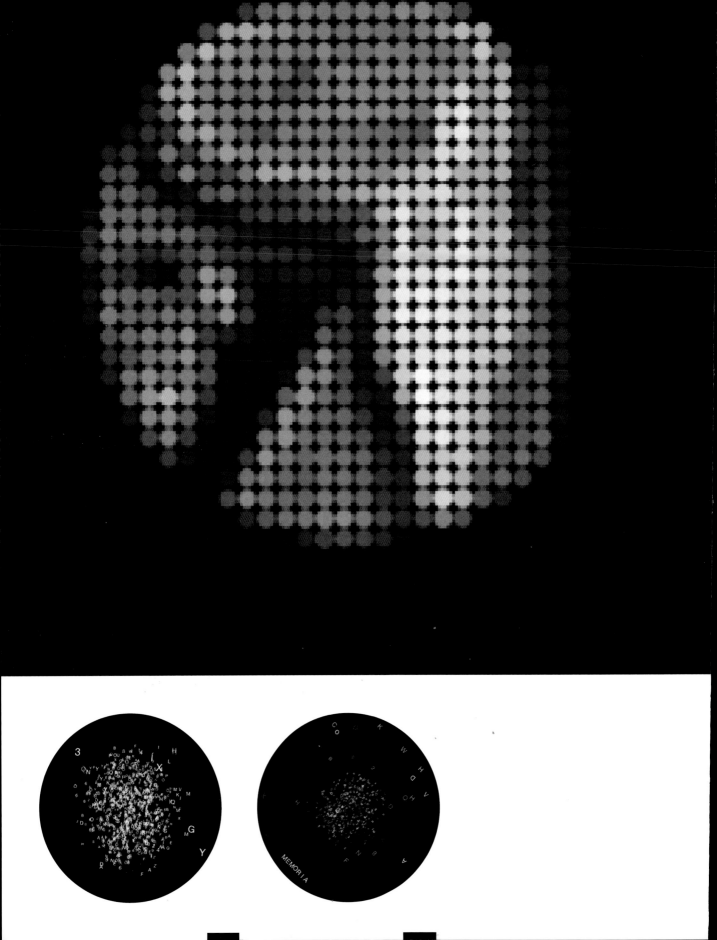

Ta Matete Il Pozzo

BITFORMS

Steve Sacks runs bitforms, a New York gallery specialising in software art. He represents a number of leading software artists, including Golan Levin, Danny Rozin, Casey Reas and Danny Brown. One of bitforms' most successful pieces to date has been the *Software Art Station*, an integrated computer processor and flat touch-screen designed to display interactive touch-screen works, compact enough to be hung on the wall, and which bears an uncanny resemblance to that most traditional of art commodities, the painting. Many of the pieces created for the *Software Art Station* can be described as "reactive painting", where the viewer creates the image by touching the screen. Sacks explains more: "I started bitforms to explore the realms of digital art. To redefine categories and levels of artistic engagement. To discover new art. To educate and share these new artistic processes with the world. The category of art that has been most challenging for bitforms to define, market and legitimise has been software art. How do you collect it? Define it? What is its value? Future value? Archivability? Maintenance? Framed works are sold as variant editions or one of a kind and are typically much higher priced than unframed. With framed works, there is complete control by the artist as to how the artwork will function and be displayed. Many times the framing or housing of the software is conceptually tied to the work. Some artists collaborate to fabricate their objects, where as others have the skill set to build the entire artwork. Software art objects need to be robust and easily maintained. Typically there is a guarantee and a detailed maintenance manual. Since there is hardware involved, care must be given to usage. At bitforms, we are adamant about how the work should be presented. We recommend a dedicated machine and monitor to run the works. To help people manage their software art, we have created an administrative tool that allows collectors to add, delete and select pieces. Once the software art is loaded and added to the system, the collector doesn't have to go back to the desktop. This is an important step in creating an isolated system that is focused on the viewing and interaction of software art.

"Collectors of this type of art vary. There are the old–school collectors who are intrigued by the work and the low entry cost. There are the new collectors who are excited about the new technologies and the interactive nature of certain works. And there are museums that want to maintain a link to what is current and new. Some common questions collectors have are: What am I actually getting? What is the artist's role? Is this really art? The collector is getting a set of rules or parameters determined by the artist. These rules are the art. They are the essence of the experience and aesthetic direction. The rules can be interpreted as the code the artist writes. The questioning of this as an art form is to be expected.

"Software art is empowering. Engaging. Endless. Whether or not it becomes a valuable collectible, I am convinced that it will be a part of the art nomenclature. Its beauty and possibilities are too alluring. The artists are too talented. And the world deserves a new creative outlet."

Cells by Casey Reas
Software Art Station

BOUTIQUE VIZIQUE

"Some four years ago, we decided to collaborate on a small video and since then we have been working side by side on multiple projects. Boutique Vizique has been a playground where we meet new friends, fool around and share our dreams. But it's also a place where we learn about software, different arts, physical laws and ourselves.

"Vizique is a contraction of the words 'visual' and 'physical' in French. Our little collective stands in the young tradition of multimedia and performance artists who are trying to close the gap between the flesh and technology in their work. Technology has become a natural ingredient in all our recent work, but that doesn't imply we can't live without it anymore. The most important thing to us is that we never use technology to express itself. It's always an instrument, a tool. In our installations, we feed our machines with a portion of the physical world and chunks of human data. We try to come up with alternative interfaces and play with different kinds of input, reconstruct a given space. Every time an answer is given, a dozen new questions arise. Probably this is what keeps us going".

Babble

"Listen! I am a machine, but nevertheless soft and stuborn. I listen to everything around me, I look at the world. Voices, noises, howling and barking, foreheads, lips, a funny face. "Look! I am looking for the heartbeat of images and sounds. I love poetry and create dreams to share them with you. I try to unite everything in little moments. Moments when everything comes together, like 'blablatickytickyribbitoink', and then, all of a sudden, an explosion – BOEM! *Babble* makes your ears listen while your face dances and jumps around. *Babble* is an audiovisual installation for kids. By pushing one of the seven buttons on a capture unit, every little visitor can record a sound and video loop (2-5 seconds). After recording, the video appears (faded and quiet) in the projection. On a separate unit, seven pressure-sensitive buttons correspond to seven 'floats' hanging from the ceiling. If nobody pushes the pressure pads, there is only a whispering in the room. All video and sound are faded. If you push a pad, the projected face on the floats will emerge clearly and the singing will become louder. By stepping on and off the pads, compositions can be made with this AV choir."
http://www.boutiquevizique.com/babble/home.html

Fritzie

"*Fritzie* the doll is lying silent in a corner. He looks comfortable, tempting to the touch, a big, huggable doll. But be careful! When you come too close, he wakes up and then whispers evil dreams – a man/machine dreaming of flesh and blood. *Fritzie* is a soft sculpture made with fabric and string. An old iMac and webcam is *Fritzie's* head, eye and voice and a Max/MSP/jitter–patch is his brain."

Drawplay

"*Drawplay* is an installation that generates audio according to one's drawing. On a computer screen, a blank area invites visitors to make a drawing by using a touch screen. The drawing is scanned vertically between editable 'in' and 'out' points. The acquired data is encoded and read out as a sound and this creates a particular mask on top of a video file. There is a correlation between the type of sketch and the sound: the higher the position of the created dots or lines, the higher the sound; continuous lines give continuous sound, dots fragmented sounds. The more one draws, the more of the projected video is revealed. The encoding of the drawing is not straightforward and therefore stimulates one's creativity. Players are challenged to draw in different ways in order to understand how they can create specific sounds."

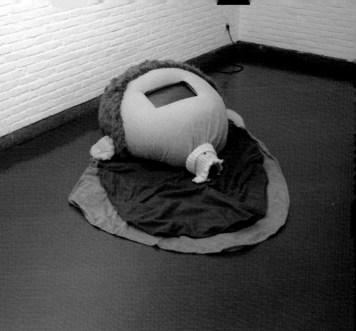

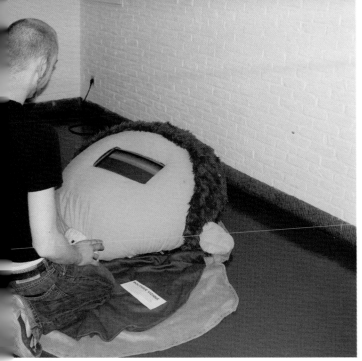

Fritzie

Babble

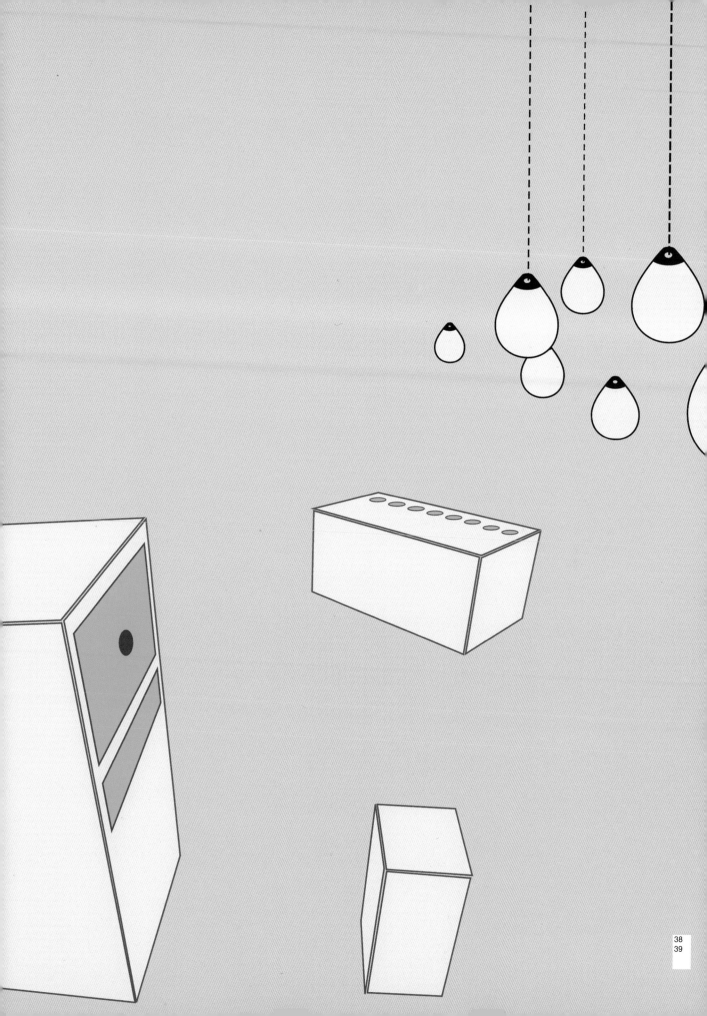

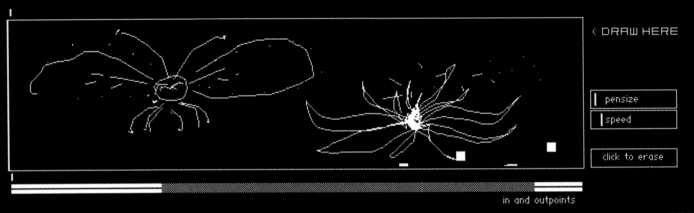

< DRAW HERE

| pensize |
| speed |
| click to erase |

in and outpoints

DRAW_PLAY >>>

Drawplay

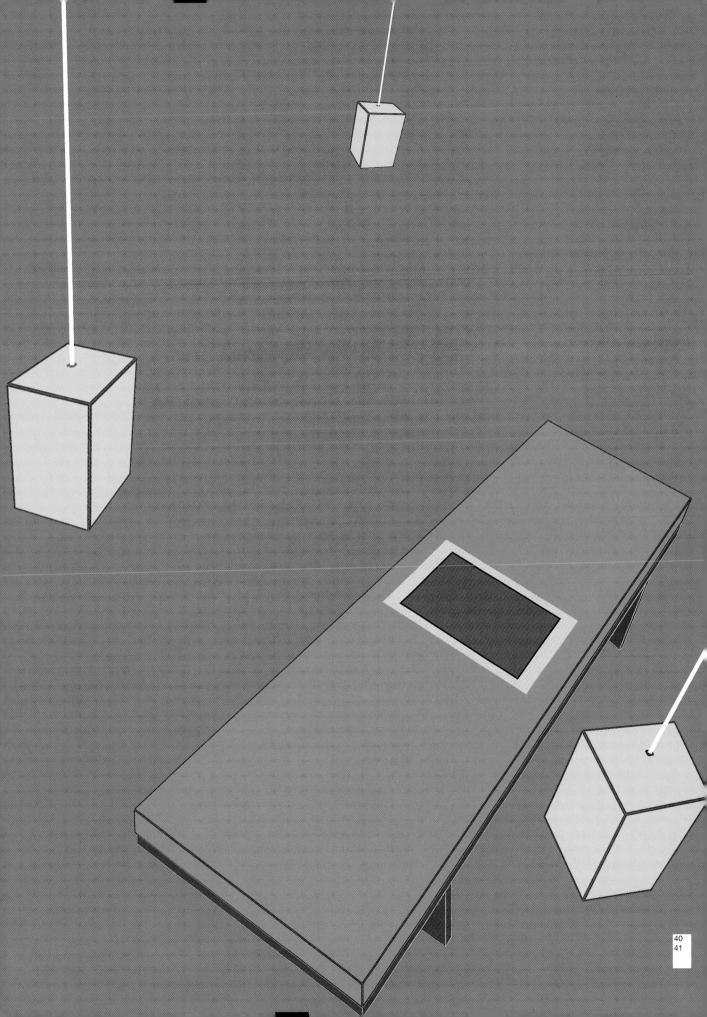

DANIEL ROZIN

Daniel Rozin is an artist, educator and developer, working in the area of interactive digital art. As an interactive artist, he creates installations and sculptures that change and respond to the presence and point of view of the viewer. In many cases the viewer becomes the contents of the piece and in others the viewer is invited to take an active role in the creation of the piece. Even though computers are often used in Rozin's work, they are seldom visible.

Of his own work, he says: "It is my belief that much of what is happening in the area of New Media and interaction design is directed and paced by technological developments of which designers are taking advantage as they are presented. The problem with such an approach is that the direction of new designs is defined by engineers who develop new technologies because they can, not necessarily because of their design impact. It has become my mission as a designer, developer and educator to try to reverse this flow. I believe that the source and inspiration for new designs should be, as it has always been, the emotions, expressions and aesthetics of people. The tools to bring these concepts to life have changed over the past centuries and are changing now; designers need to be able to use and develop the new tools and language necessary for their expression."

Shiny Balls Mirror

"Shiny Balls Mirror is a large physical object made of 900 hollow metal tubes with polished chrome balls placed in them. The whole piece has the form of a large hexagon. Each hollow tube and shiny ball are one pixel in the display. This pixel has the ability to change its brightness by moving the chrome ball in (darker) or out (brighter) of the tube. The display serves as a mirror in the way it reflects the viewer as a whole, but also in the way it reflects the viewer 900 times on the shiny balls, making the positive content of the display (the bright pixels) the viewers themselves.

Trash Mirror and Wooden Mirror

"Trash Mirror is made of 500 pieces of trash collected between February and June 2002 on the streets of New York. These pieces were flattened and connected to motors, and with the help of a computer they are orchestrated to reflect whoever stands in front of the piece. From afar, the image of the reflected person can be vividly observed while the contents of the trash cannot. Up close, the trash becomes visible and interesting, while the image is too coarse to be comprehended. As the trash pieces have irregular shapes, the surface is very different from the orderly X by Y grid that is used for digital displays and they do not come through as pixels; instead, the piece celebrates the ability of computation to make sense of and orchestrate even the messiest of substances. Because the trash that comprises the surface of this piece has many shades and colours and varies in shape and size, the computer needs to be extra smart to decide how to move each piece in order to create the best reflection of the viewer. To do so, the computer has to have a very intimate knowledge of every piece of trash. In fact, the first stage of programming the Trash Mirror involved having the computer teach itself the exact placement of each piece by pointing a video camera at the piece itself rather than the viewer."

Me-rror

"The Me-rror is an interactive mirror that follows whoever is in front of it. The result is that anyone standing in front of the Me-rror sees themselves reflected in all of the mirror strips simultaneously . The Me-rror tracks the person in front of it and changes its state to accommodate their position. If two people stand in front of the Me-rror, the response changes, and the Me-rror changes its state so that each person sees the other person in all 20 strips.

"The Me-rror is on display at the Interactive Telecommunications Program area at NYU in a busy corridor where it follows the students as they walk in. and out of the classrooms."

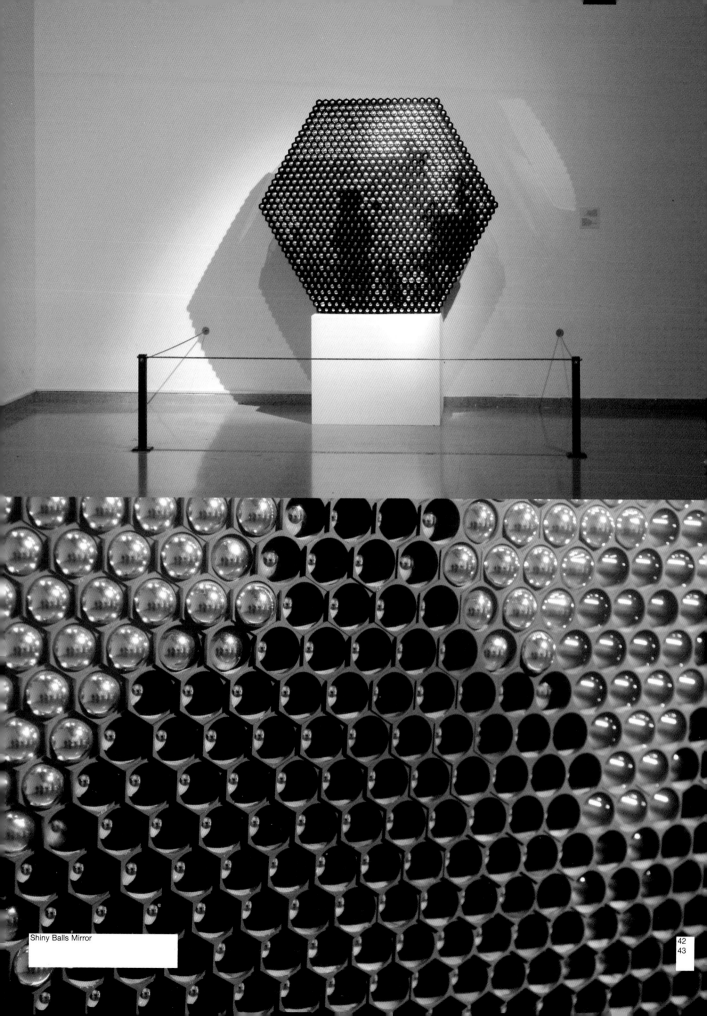

Shiny Balls Mirror

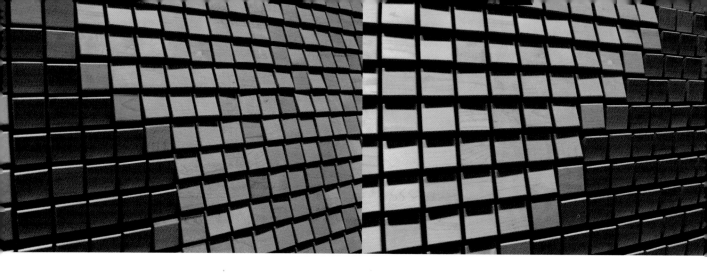

Wooden Mirror

Trash Mirror

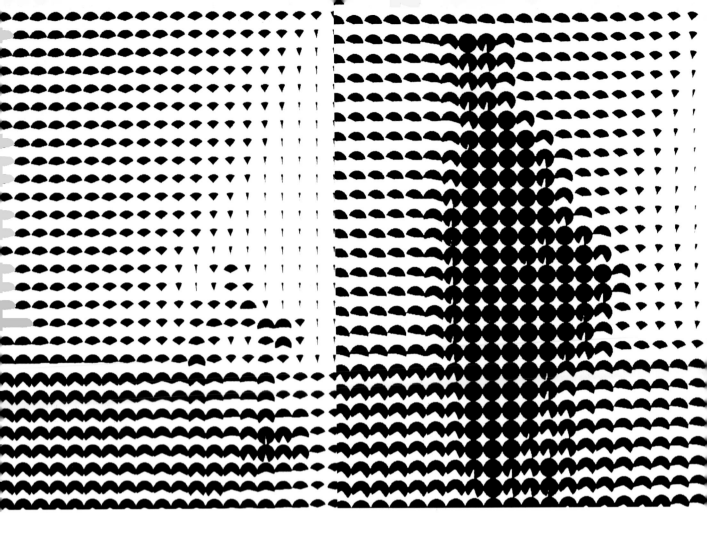

Software Mirror

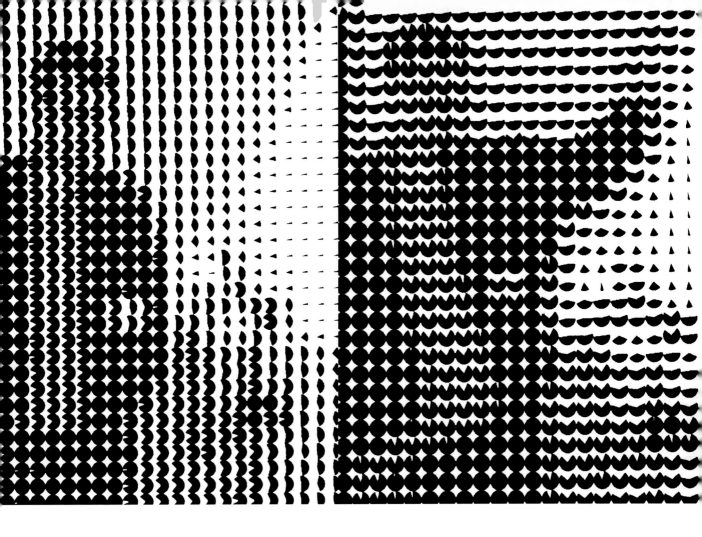

Me-rror

DELAWERE

Delaware, in its own words, is "a Japanese supersonic group that designs rock and rocks design". Its leading members are Masato Samata, Aya Honda, Morihiro Tajiri and Yoshiki Watanabe. Asked what its main activity is, the communal answer comes back: "Works/activities include everything from music CDs and CD-ROMs to TV commercials, magazines, T-shirts, websites, mobile phones, cross–stitching and live shows." Its website *freeware/delaware*, with "horizontal scroll", has attracted the attention of designers around the world, it claims.
www.delaware.gr.jp

Asked about its cult hit song *HMS In The Rain*, the group spokesperson says: "The song is actually *Designin 'In The Rain from Delaware Strikes Back*. It is composed by Yoshiki Watanabe, lyrics by Samata, arranged by Tajiri, vocal by Aya Honda – so all the members of Delaware cooperated in this song and they all like it."

Designin' In The Rain (lyrics)
I am designin' in the rain,
Just graphic-designin' in the rain.
Red, yellow, green, blue, black and white,
Stripe, check, bitmap, free-freehand,
Brightness and contrast, colour balance.
Like a James Brown, like a haiku.
I am designin' in the rain,
Just graphic-designin' in the rain.
Air beat, shit deep, yeah, enough jean
Ouch eye jar hey hell amp end
Oh peep cool ah essay tea woo
Beer dub tax wine zzzziiiiiiiiiiit.
Red, yellow, green, blue, black and white,
Stripe, check, bitmap, free-freehand,
Brightness and contrast, colour balance,
Just graphic–designin' in the rain.

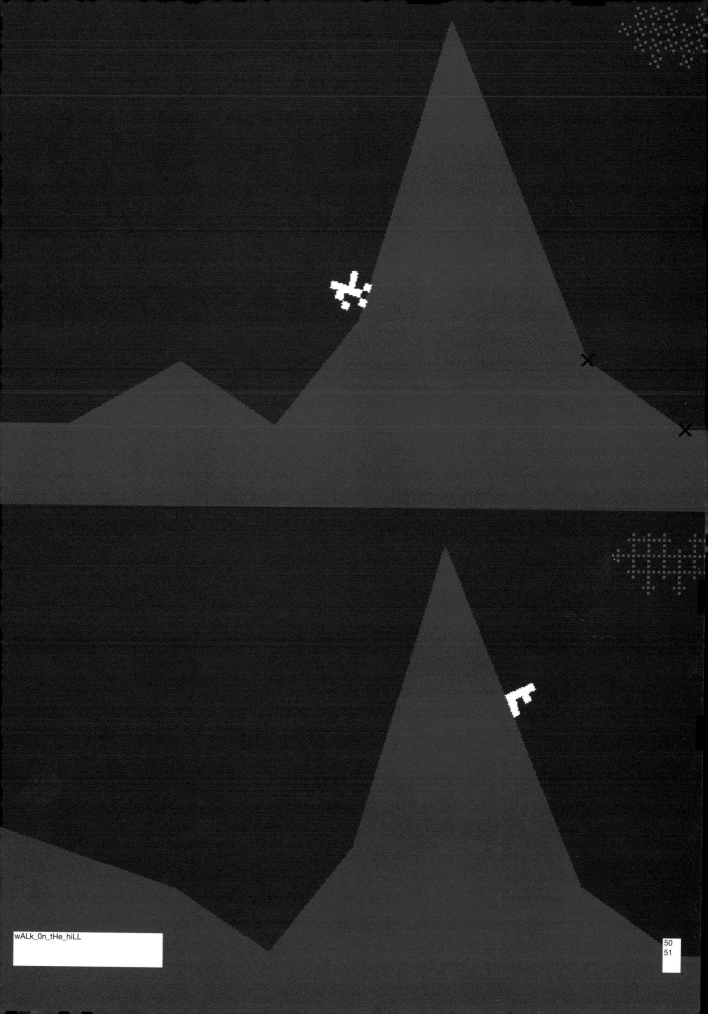

wALk_0n_tHe_hiLL

hms_iN_tHe_rAiN

DIGIT

Daljit Singh explains the philosophy behind Digit. "Collaboration is fundamental to progression. I want us to be working hand-in-hand with designers from diverse fields to make creative but useful devices for hotels, cars and related technologies. We've always put great emphasis on R&D and our past investment in experimental work is now coming to fruition. By allowing our designers to push the boundaries of interaction and interface design, we've been able to inspire clients by exposing them to more progressive ideas. When we were smaller we had quite a structured system that devoted Wednesday afternoons to experimenting – rather like sports afternoons at school! Digit has been able to strategically exploit its past investment in these projects through promotion of the work and exhibiting it at leading galleries and museums. We're now reaping the benefits by being frequently commissioned to develop exciting bespoke installations for new and existing clients."

MotoGlyph

"*MotoGlyph* was created for the exclusive nightly 'Sunset Sessions' in Miami. Guests could create their own digital signature with a customised optical pen. The variables of marks and strokes were translated by the system into sound and animation. Users could then download an MP3 of their ringtone to their mobile from www.hellomoto.com/motoglyph."

Thinking Fish

"The concept of *Thinking Fish* is to have a fish tank where real fish are augmented with mind bubbles above their heads. When the fish swim around in the tank, the bubbles follow. Colour tracking is used to distinguish between the different fish in the aquarium, and the mind bubbles are projected onto the back wall of the tank accordingly.

"The project plays with the idea of mixing realities where information technology is given a more ambient role in a physical setting. Since this is work in progress, the interaction with the fish has not been finally decided yet. But the idea is that spectator should be able to interact with the fish using a mobile phone – voice call, SMS and Bluetooth are some of the technologies we are considering for communicating with the fish."

The Digital Aquarium.

"One hundred and fifty Motorola phones were suspended as part of an audio-visual installation in London's Design Museum Tank. The installation was brought to life whenever a passer-by dialled one of the mobile phone numbers posted up on *The Digital Aquarium* tank. Each number related to a series of patterns that triggered off a chain reaction as the signal travelled from phone to phone, creating a shimmering effect of fish swimming around an aquarium as each mobile lit up, vibrated and rang in a pre-programmed sequence."

Digital Aquarium

MotoGlyph

EAR STUDIO INC

Mark Hansen is a statistician at Bell Labs and Ben Rubin is multimedia artist and sound designer. They talk about *Listening Post*, an installation which scans online chat and transforms into music.

"Anyone who types a message in a chat room and hits 'send' is calling out for a response. *Listening Post* is our response – a series of soundtracks and visual arrangements of text that reflect the scale, the immediacy, and the meaning in a dynamic, global conversation.

"The advent of online communication has created a vast landscape of new spaces for public discourse: chat rooms, bulletin boards and scores of other public on-line forums. While these spaces are public and social in their essence, the experience of 'being in' such a space is silent and solitary. A participant in a chat room has limited sensory access to the collective 'buzz' of that room or of others nearby – the murmur of human contact that we hear naturally in a park, a plaza or a coffee shop is absent from the online experience. The goal of *Listening Post* is to collect this buzz and render it at a human scale. *Listening Post* draws on real-time exchanges from tens of thousands of on-line forums. We use sound, text, motion and space to create sensual encounters with this data, abstracting the communication spaces away from their familiar on-screen presence. Taken together, public on-line communications represent an enormous outpouring of real-time data, and this data is filled with complex structure. Topics emerge in response to current events and daily activities in cycles that vary hour-to-hour, day-to-day and season-to-season. Emerging issues transcend the boundaries of the on-line landscape: a local knitting circle in Australia and a political discussion group on Yahoo may both react to news of a political scandal or a World Cup victory.

"Our goal is to distill the content and the structure of this collective communication and to present it in ways that are accessible and compelling. Every word that enters our system was typed only seconds before by someone, somewhere. The irregular staccato of these arriving messages form the visual and audible rhythms of the work. The sound-generating systems are constructed almost as wind chimes, where the wind in this case is not meteorological but human, and the particles that move are not air molecules but thoughts and words. *Listening Post* is about harnessing the human energy that is carried by all of these words and channeling that energy through the mechanisms of the piece."

Listening Post

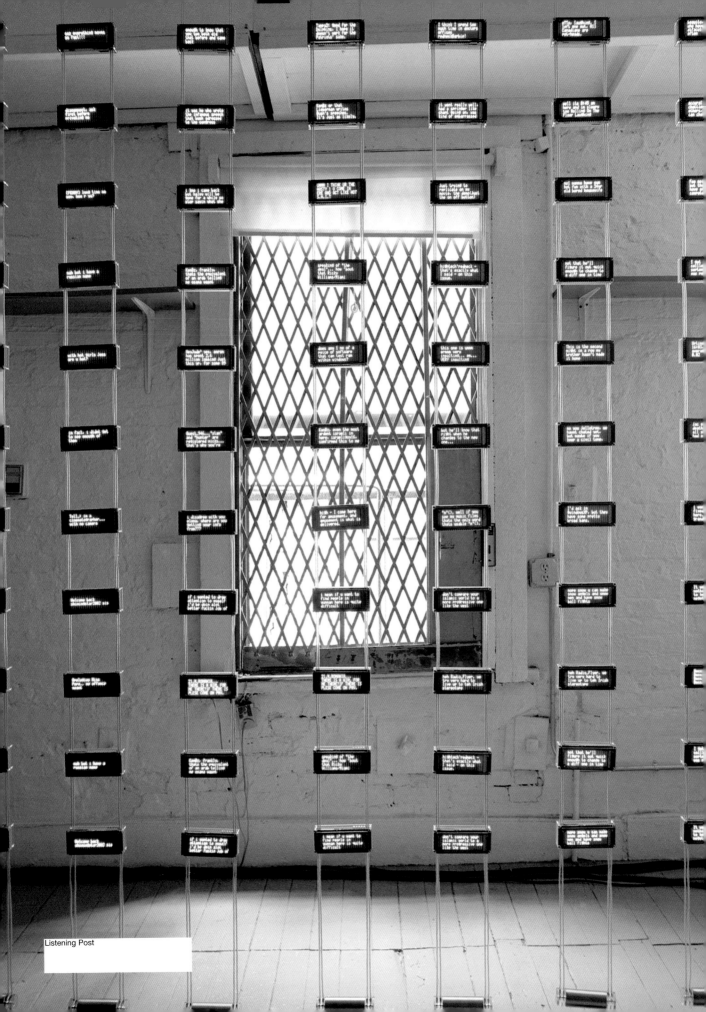

Listening Post

FABRICA

Fabrica is the Benetton Centre for Communication Research in Treviso, Italy. It is a unique institution, part agency, part research institute, part art school, housed in an extraordinary modernist building by Tadao Ando. Fabrica's mission is to come up with original and innovative creative solutions in design, photography, video, writing, visual communication and interactive media. To this end, it invites the pick of young international talent to spend one year in Italy working on a range of commercial and non–commercial projects.

(Editor's note: At this point I must declare a personal interest – I am Creative Director of Interactive at Fabrica.)

United People

United People is a video messaging system for Benetton megastores. Customers use a touch-screen Macintosh computer to send video messages to friends, search the video database and send videos back to anyone on-line who catches their eye. It is a playful project that reinforces Benetton's reputation for leading the way in new strategies of communication. It's also a serious exploration of how e-mail, mobile telephony, on-line chat and reality TV are changing the nature of marketing and advertising.

Petri Saariko explains more ..." The original idea was to create a global communication medium utilising the Benetton brand where ideas of communication and self–reflection could be questioned in a continuous flux of visual communication. We took the whole Benetton brand onto the next level to reflect our views about the Internet age. Benetton advertising has always been about multiculturalism and people – what we wanted to do was to replace colourful photo models from around the world with real people from around the world. And it worked!" Andrea Masiero adds "The energy and spontaneity of the videos we get is amazing. Some people are very creative. It's really a lot of fun to watch."

United People will be extended to Benetton stores in 11 more cities in mid 2004 including Bombay, Shanghai and Istanbul

Dare

"*Dare* is a interactive installation in which visitors to the show become the authors of the show. Four touch-screens running four artworks – *Grid*, *Face*, *Draw* and *Model* – invite the audience to record their gestures and expressions in real time. Everything is saved to disk with a date and time stamp. The artwork grows over time into a complex and almost musical sequence of visual rhythm and counterpoint.

"Because it keeps a record of everything that happens within it, *Dare* is both an interactive artwork and a form of documentation – a sort of narrative of its own creation. The visitor can choose to play for him/herself, or watch a sequence created by others. *Dare* is concerned with time and authorship, and the way these define the difference between two forms of representation – the game and the story. It connects the 'now' of play with the 'then' of narrative and so blurs the line between artist and audience."

Q

In *Q*, water is the interface. The player dips his or her hand into a glass tank full of water and swirls it round and around to create waves. The waves are picked up by sensors inside the tank, which instruct a computer to generate musical sounds and 3D patterns of light – which are projected back into the water. "What I think works with *Q* is its hybridity – it is not really under the control of the user. You create waves with your hand but you can never be sure of getting the same result twice, the waves are unpredictable. So you feel as if you have partial control of a natural system. It goes against the mainstream of interaction design, which is about aiming for perfect control. It is a liquid installation of an abstract thought, a machine that behaves unlike a machine."
– Francesco Meneghini

Sound Input

In 2003, Yugo Nakamura visited Fabrica to do a workshop on sound-input interactivity. Ross Phillips explains his sound input toy *Lines*. "Tom Jennings sent me these lines and I initially had them lined up behind a grid to create a moiré pattern. It was very nice, but very technical-looking and very black and white. I wanted to make something a bit more cheerful so I stripped out the grid from the foreground to make a very obvious connection between the sound and the graphic."

Drew Allen talks about *Cylinder*, another sound input toy from the same workshop "*Cylinder* grew out of a desire to create truly complex objects, taking the sometimes minute fluctuations in sound pressure which we experience as background noise or music and rendering them in a tangible and permanent manner, as sculptures representing a sample of time."

DARE Grid
DARE Draw

United People

Sound Input Lines

Sound Input Cylinder

FROG DESIGN

Frog Design's latest interactive environment was done for the Amore Pacific flagship store in Soho, New York, in collaboration with Golan Levin and Zach Lieberman. It is described thus: "Amore Pacific is the largest manufacturer of cosmetics in South Korea. This installation consists of a 30-foot interactive projection wall. Products are displayed on a marble shelf, with water slowly flowing across the stone surface. The projection system displays a real-time, software-generated environment of ripples in water. As a customer walks by the counter, inspirational words appear in the projection above each product grouping. These words respond to the dynamics of the virtual ripples and slowly wash away as the customer continues to walk through the store. A wake of ripples is left as customers walk back and forth. If the customer stops in front of a product grouping, then more detailed information appears, highlighting the benefits of those products. The text display is large enough to be legible to other customers who might be elsewhere in the store.

"The entire system is delivered through two PCs, four digital projectors and two video cameras, which provide the computer vision. The store opened to the public in early August last year, but was drawing evening crowds on the sidewalk even prior to the opening, as people stopped to stare at the projection wall."

ENERGIZE PROTECT RESTORE

serum moisturizers
& eye care

FIRM RENEW REFINE

line modification
& special care

Amore Pacific

FUTUREFARMERS

"Cultivating your consciousness," since 1995, Futurefarmers is a group of artists based in San Francisco. Amy Franceschini, the group's founder, talks about four of its recent interactive projects.

Intro To Game Theory

"A table was placed on the floor in a gallery space. Three people were asked at random to play the game and three rules were assigned, but given as open to change. Over the course of the night, the game evolved from an 'age three-plus' board game to an intricate building-block, sound-mixing, multi-dimensional toy. "How does it work? A camera was mounted to the ceiling and connected to a computer. The grid area of the game was tracked by the camera and each quadrant was assigned its own tone, so as game pieces were placed in the grid area, different tones were triggered. I wanted to research the nature of the game by looking at how board games provide an interface for social interaction. The board game revealed several human desires – the desire to create meaning, competition, creativity, and collaboration/team building. I think the best games are those that can be built upon and personalized with one's own meanings and stories. As to whether or not a game can be art, of course it can. But I think it also may be constructive to ask: 'Can art be a game?'

"The game was presented as an open template and tool-set with a base set of variables and rules. It was an experiment to see how players would define the game themselves, giving it meaning, rules and developing a language with the visual elements available. I, as the artist, became an observer in this experiment, documenting how players interact, and become more open to collaboration/cooperation, when they become the authors of the rules of the game."

Fingerprint Maze

"It starts with a physical interface that scans people's fingerprints. It uses custom software to translate the fingerprint scan into a 3D model maze that one can wander through on screen. Each individual fingerprint maze is graced by the presence of an extinct animal as a 3D rendering or animation. There is, of course, a reference to bio-security issues, but that is not the impetus of the project. In fact, the project is in part a reaction to the fear/paranoia factors surrounding bio-security issues. It is more a look at the wonders of the personal pattern that decorates the underside of your hand. *Fingerprint Maze* looks at the human fingerprint in terms of the unique mark it has left on the globe environmentally."

Homeland Security Blanket

"A small run of *Homeland Security Blankets* were made shortly after the US invaded Iraq. The blankets were to be telematically controlled and would react to the fluctuating 'threat level' of the Homland Advisory System. As a means to 'disseminate information', these blankets disseminate temperature change and an indicating light that alerts the user to current threat and comforts them accordingly."

Concurrently

"*Concurrently* is a window into global news – live, streaming news from each continent. The project was inspired by a newsstand I saw while travelling in Turkey. The cover of the paper depicted Clinton as a devil with horns and the headline read, "SATAN". I quickly ran up to the newsstand to find out the reference and discovered that while I had been away the whole Clinton/Lewinsky ordeal had gone down. News is stripped from *The Times* of London, *Le Monde* and the BBC online sites to stream into the Europe browser. News from *The New York Times*, *Los Angeles Times* and many other American online news sites is streamed into the browser designed for America. Each browser is accompanied by a 3D newscaster/bot. These 3D personalities present news in animated sequences that are interrupted not by advertisements, but two random animations: a sea of swimming fish and an animated city locator map."

"... for although in a certain sense and for light-minded persons, non-existent things can be more easily and irresponsibly represented in words than existing things, for the serious and conscientious historian it is just the reverse. Nothing is harder, yet nothing is more necessary than to speak of certain things whose existence is neither demonstratable nor probable. The very fact that serious and conscientious men treat them as existing things brings them a step closer to existence and to the possibility of being born."
– Albert Secundus (from The Glass Bead Game by Herman Hesse).

Concurrently

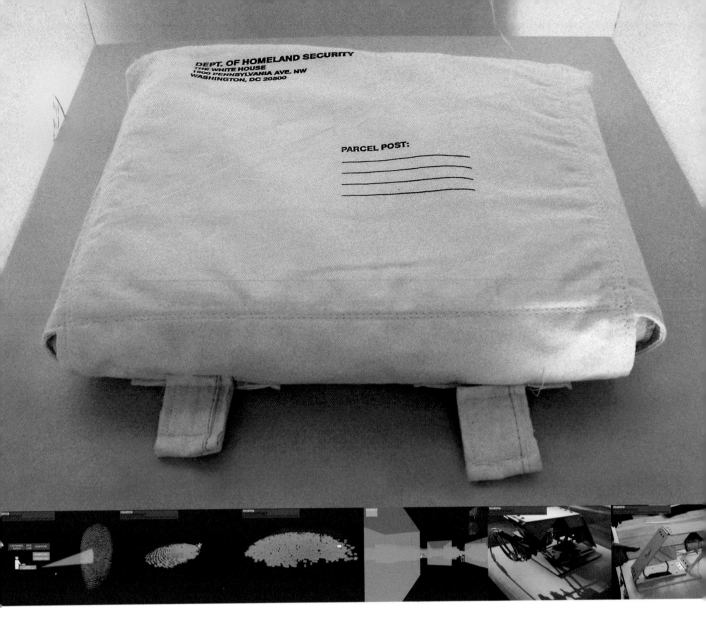

Homeland Security Blanket

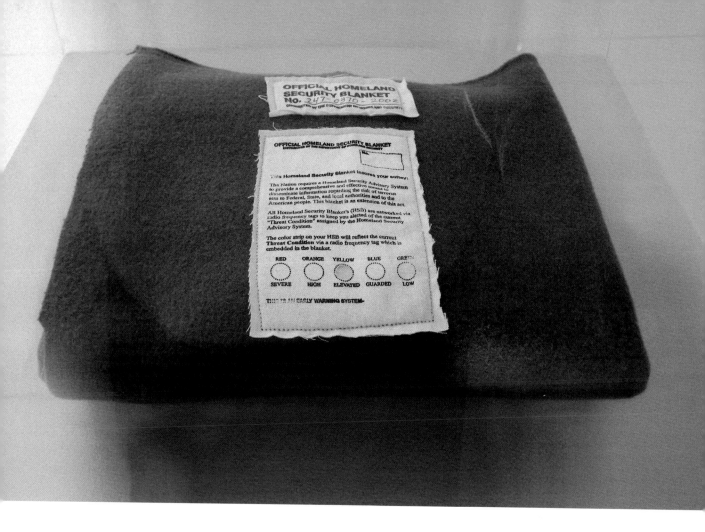

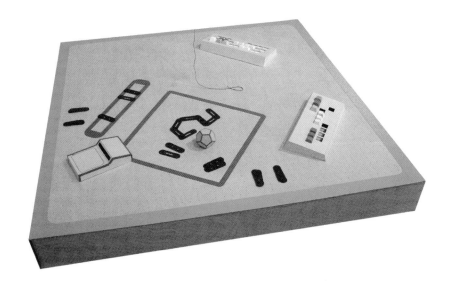

Fingerprint Maze

GOLAN LEVIN AND ZACH LIEBERMAN, TMEMA

Tmema is a partnership between Golan Levin and Zach Lieberman, based in New York City, and their assorted collaborators. Levin writes: "Tmema initially grew out of an invitation I received to create a massively networked virtual-reality installation for the Ars Electronica Center in Linz. I knew this project would be too big to make on my own, so I invited my best student Zach to come along and help out. I taught him everything I know. Well, Zach graduated and nowadays, it's him who teaches me." Tmema has worked on a variety of artistic and commercial projects, including interactive point-of-purchase displays, museum installations and avant-garde performances.

Messa di Voce

"*Messa di Voce* (Italian for 'placing the voice') is a concert performance in which the speech, shouts and songs produced by two vocalists are radically augmented in real time by custom interactive visualisation software. The performance touches on themes of abstract communication, synaesthetic relationships, cartoon language and writing and scoring systems, within the context of a sophisticated, playful, and virtuosic audiovisual narrative. Tmema's software transforms every vocal nuance into correspondingly complex, subtly differentiated and highly expressive graphics. These visuals not only depict the singers' voices, but also serve as controls for their acoustic playback. While the voice-generated graphics thus become an instrument that the singers can perform on, body-based manipulations of these graphics additionally replay the sounds of the singers' voices – thus creating a cycle of interaction that fully integrates the performers into an ambience consisting of sound, virtual objects and real-time processing. *Messa di Voce* lies at an intersection of human and technological performance extremes, melding the unpredictable spontaneity and extended vocal techniques of two master composer-improvisers with the latest in computer-vision and speech-analysis technologies. Utterly wordless, yet profoundly verbal, *Messa di Voce* is designed to provoke questions about the meaning and effects of speech sounds, speech acts, and the immersive environment of language."
http://tmema.org/messa/messa.html

Independently, Levin has also made forays into the belly of the New York City art world. Since 2001, he has been represented by the bitforms Gallery in Manhattan's chic Chelsea district. bitforms provides a forum to display some of the most vibrant and relevant art being made today, offering collectors an opportunity to discover a range of original and innovative forms. At bitforms, Levin sells 'software artworks' in limited editions of 100 or 200 copies. Collectors who purchase these works frequently display them on dedicated plasma screens or large, wall-mounted LCDs.

Floccus

"In 1999, I began to study the means by which dynamic graphical lines might become able to convey a plausible sense of physicality. I developed a model for representing the underlying structure of 'physical' lines, in which a finite-element, mass-spring-damper simulation is composed of virtual particles connected by alternating linear and torsional springs. The model has the effect of simulating the tensile properties of thin physical filaments, such as hairs or twigs. I used this physical model to create two reactive drawing systems, *Brillo* and *Floccus*.
"In *Floccus* (the Latin term for 'hairball'), ductile filaments drawn by the user swirl around a shifting, imaginary drain centered at the user's cursor. These filaments – torn by conflicting impulses to simultaneously preserve their length, yet also move towards or away from the cursor – find an equilibrium by forming gnarly, tangled masses. *Floccus* is sonified in real time by a custom software granular synthesizer."

The Alphabet Synthesis Machine (2001)

"This is an online artwork that allows one to create and evolve the possible writing systems of imaginary civilizations. The abstract alphabets produced by the machine can be downloaded as TrueType fonts, and are compiled in an archive of user creations. The results probe the liminal territories between familiarity and chaos, language and gesture.
"Shown here are examples of alphabets created with the *Alphabet Synthesis Machine*, and a physical installation of the machine created for the bitforms gallery. The machine can be seen online at http://alphabet.tmema.org/."

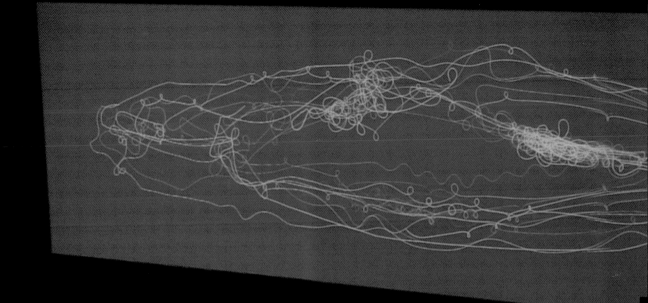

Floccus

Messa di Voce

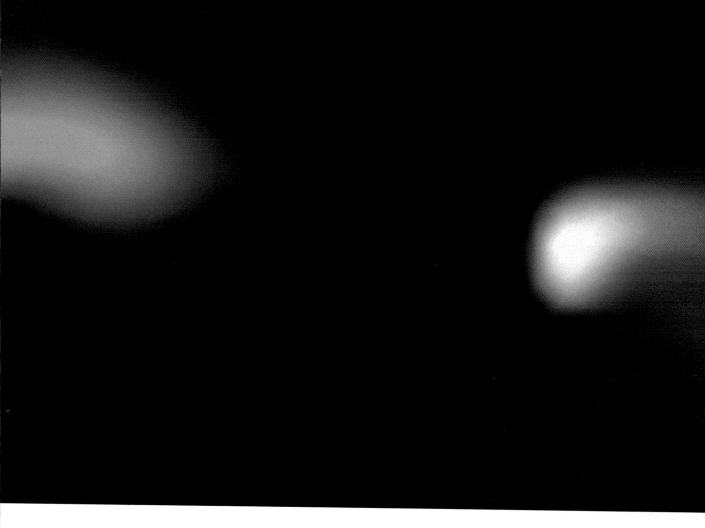

The Alphabet Synthesis Machine

GRAHAME WEINBREN

Grahame Weinbren has set himself the task of re-conceiving cinema as an interactive experience. He has developed technologies and interfaces, hardware and software, to make it possible for his works to be different for each viewer who encounters them. For 20 years he has explored a variety of non-linear cinematic structures, including narratives, documentaries and game-like works. Each piece is presented in its own environment and uses a different technique for interacting with the screen.

The Erl King

"*The Erl King*, made in collaboration with Roberta Friedman, was produced in the early 1980s and exhibited extensively from 1985 to 1991. Originally it was an analog piece that stored its video material on three laser-disc players controlled by a Z80 8Mhz computer running two floppy discs. Viewers could navigate through about two hours of moving images, shot in 16mm film.

"The images included a performance of the Schubert/Goethe high Romantic German lied *Erlkoenig*, and a reenactment of a dream described by Freud in which child's dead body bursts into flame. The song was sung in German, and viewers could access the translation on screen – each line was spray-painted on a car that had been abandoned along the edges of Manhattan.

"*The Erl King* combines both high and low culture crammed into a small interactive screen – along with Schubert and grafittied automobiles, there are chickens dyed primary colours followed by an operating chicken-feather-plucking machine, improvising trombonists, a gospel group, a Chinese chef, a Hawaiian shirt collection, a Lacanian psychoanalyst and much more. A viewer navigates through this jungle by means of a touch screen: there are other screens on which an audience can watch without interacting.

The Erl King has just been acquired by the Guggenheim Museum and has been transformed into an all-digital work that runs on a single computer."

Sonata

"*Sonata* (1991-93) is a narrative piece, based on the biblical story of Judith decapitating Holofernes to save her home town and Tolstoy's novella *The Kreutzer Sonata*, about an aristocrat who stabs his wife to death because he suspects her of infidelity. Participants can look at each story from multiple points of view, by pointing at a projection screen, and navigate through the dense imagery as if they were in a dream. The stories interweave and overlap, but keep moving forward towards the inevitable murder scenes. There is also a large database of cinematic material available, and though all journeys through the piece lead to the same places, the possible routes to the endings are almost infinitely variable."

Frames

"*Frames* (1999) expands to multiple channels. Commissioned by the ICC Media Museum in Tokyo, it is a three–screen work, which two viewers can operate at once. Viewers point through gilded, empty frames, lined with infrared sensors, at very large projections, trying to transform contemporary young women into 19th-century 'mad women'. The performers have modelled their characters on the first asylum-patient photographs taken by Hugh Diamond in the 1840s. One of the ideas of the work is to link the most recent technologies with the breakthrough technology of 150 years ago, black-and-white photography. *Frames* is a narrative with a game-like structure and requires collaboration between the two "players": both attempt to transform their characters simultaneously. If they succeed, they are rewarded with an on-screen encounter between the mad women, which is in most cases quite unpredictable and bizarre."

Sonata
Erl King

Frames

IDEO

O2 Message Wall

When the British mobile telephone company O2 opened a flagship retail store on London's Oxford Street in 2003, they wanted a space combining technology and art where customers would stay, learn and play. They invited IDEO to design a distinctive wall display on a two-storey wall of the interior of the store for carrying messages, greetings, product and service announcements and offers. The final design takes the form of amoebic 'bubbles' which are mounted on a wall 5 metres wide and 7 metres tall in an L-shape. The bubbles displays information in graphic and text form which flows in patterns of fluid motion from one display to the next through more than 5300 LED's.

Durrell Bishop adds "O2 saw the display system we did at the Science Museum in London and they really liked it, but we didn't want to do the same job again. What we were interested in doing was taking the LED off the grid. When you do this it starts to get really interesting visually, in terms of what your eyes expect and what they actually see. It is quite striking. We did the software in house, both the low level pic code and the PC controlling code. The key to the whole thing is having a networked display controller – we created a whole number of models or 'compositions' of the way text can move from one display to another. This could be a really good way of thinking about large scale architectural display systems in the future – you could wrap a lot of them around a building and each display would know its place in the sequence, like an intelligent alternative to the billboard or jumbotron."

02 Message Wall

LANDESIGN

Landesign is a design consultancy formed in 1992. Landesign's best known project was the Play Zone at The Millennium Dome in London.

Urbis

"Land has developed two of the four galleries set within *Urbis*, a structure that investigates the concept of the modern city. The objective was to help demystify and assist in understanding wide-ranging personal relationships with the city by using Manchester as a portal to other cultures and situations on a global scale. *Change* uses a range of interactive situations to consider how people influence and are influenced by the city they call home. Life-sized people pods and a bespoke 'blue screen' sequence engage the visitor with real people and their actual city. "*Explore* is encountered through an award-winning module that provides a unique interface enabling access to an extensive database exploring how people have imagined the city. Beyond this, *Urbisville* presents a self-styled matrix that investigates the diversity and compelling narratives of six cities and five themes. This finale intentionally encourages a free-flow movement system".
www.urbis.org.uk

The Famous Grouse Experience

"The complete re-development of this Visitor Centre was undertaken by Land in 2000. Seismic floor sensors combined with a series of six computer-processed data projectors enable groups to splash through digital water, crack digital ice and fly across ever-evolving Scottish landscapes. Once the eight-minute show is complete, the management of the movement sequence delivers the pulsed group directly into the refurbished shop and restaurant".
www.famousgrouse.com

The Famous Grouse Experience
Urbis

RAFAEL LOZANO-HEMMER

Rafael Lozano–Hemmer is an interactive artist whose medium is light and shadow. His two great series – *Vectorial Elevations* and *Body Movies* – both give his audience the opportunity to intervene on a monumental scale within the city by controlling powerful projectors linked to computers.

Body Movies

Body Movies was premiered in Rotterdam in 2001 and subsequently toured worldwide. will be in Manhattan, New York City in 2004.

Body Movies throws an enormous projection of human figures onto the side of a building in a public square. This monumental image is 'burned out' by an arc light situated halfway between the image projector and the wall. By standing between the arc light and the wall, the spectator/player can create a shadow that reveals the projected image. If the spectator/player moves his or her shadow to match or 'embody' a figure in the projected image, image-analysis software recognises the match and switchesthe projected figure for the next image. By embodying figures in this way, the audience moves the sequence forward.

Rafael Lozano-Hemmer explains more: "Body Movies was inspired by Samuel van Hoogstraten's engraving *The Shadow Dance*, which appears in his *Inleiding tot de Hogeschool der Schilderkunst*. Made in Rotterdam in 1675, this engraving shows a minute source of light placed at ground level and the shadows of actors taking on demonic or angelic characteristics depending on their size. Before proposing the piece, I read Victor Stoichita's wonderful book *A Short History Of The Shadow*, where he outlines different relationships to shadows in art: the shadow as a metaphor for being (Plato), the birth of representation and painting (Butades' daughter), the mysterious expression of the self (shadowgrammes) and, most important, the expression of a hidden monstrosity or otherness (which is depicted in van Hoogstraten's engraving). So my initial desire was to use artificial shadows to generate questions about embodiment and disembodiment, about spectacular representation, about the distance between bodies in public space, and so on. It is clear that those are my obsessions and most people participating in the piece probably are reflecting on something completely different, which is great. I want to design anti-monuments. A monument is something that represents power, or selects a piece of history and tries to materialise it, visualise it, represent it, always from the point of view of the elite. The anti–monument on the contrary is an action, a performance. Everybody is aware of its artificiality. There is no inherent connection between the site and the installation. It's something that people may partake in, ad hoc, knowing it's a deceit, a special effect. The anti–monument, for me, is an alternative to the fetish of the site, the fetish of the representation of power."

Vectorial Elevations

Vectorial Elevations connected 18 powerful robotic searchlights situated on the tops of buildings around the largest square in Mexico City with an interactive 3D model on the Internet. Visitors to the website could configure the searchlights into patterns. Every eight seconds, the searchlights moved into a new configuration. Rafael Lozano-Hemmers explains more: "On a clear night, the searchlight beams could be seen from a 20km radius and covered the entire historic centre of the city, including landmarks such as the Metropolitan Cathedral, the Supreme Court of Justice and the Templo Mayor Aztec ruins. Despite the power of the installation, my intention was not to do a cathartic millennium show, but a quiet, slowly fluctuating space for reflection."

The Shadow Dance by Samuel van
Hoogstraten

Body Movies

Vectorial Elevations

RCA

The Royal College of Art has been developing and nurturing new talent in interaction design since 1990. Here are four projects from recent years. All use real time data – sound or video – and play with the time base.

TapTap

"*TapTap* is a construction toy for those fascinated with rhythm and fidgeting. It is built out of individual knock boxes. Each box has its own memory and is completely self-contained. As you tap on the top of a box, the box waits for a few seconds and then taps back what it has heard, but only once. If you want more you add another box, and another, and another, tap, tap, tap, tap, tap. Stacking the boxes creates longer and more complex rhythm lines as the patterns tumble down the resulting pyramids. "By tapping for longer than the delay period, you play a duet with the box as it repeats your earlier rhythms. The boxes themselves do not learn or loop, they only repeat. There is only tap, pause and tap. At four seconds, the delay is just long enough to give the boxes a life of their own, just long enough to wonder if they have forgotten."
– Andy Huntington and Louise Klinker

Parallel

"*Parallel* started as an investigation of what would happen if flat images were placed into a three-dimensional space. Initial experimentation yielded some interesting results, mainly when consecutive, slightly transparent images were arranged in such a way that they seemed to merge. As experimentation continued, I found that if the arrangement of images was spun fast, enough a simple animation effect emerged, similar to an early animation device, the kinescope."
– Joel Gethin Lewis

Audio Shaker

"The *Audio Shaker* explores our perceptual understanding of sound. Anything sung, spoken, clapped, whistled or played near it is trapped inside, where it takes on an imagined yet tangible physicality. Sounds caught in this void are transformed, given weight and permanance, reacting directly to the shaker's movements, subtle or violent. Shaken sounds have to settle down before becoming still and silent, behaving more like fluid than transient energy. The linear time-scale of sound is broken, a conversation is split into words and mixed up in the *Audio Shaker*, and can be poured out separately, tipped out in a simultaneous spalsh or added to and shaken up further. Put simply, it is a tactile container to capture, shake up and pour out sounds. Creating a rich, intuitive experience that is purposefully open to interpretation and imagination."
– Tom Jenkins and Mark Hauenstein

Loopqoob

'I use the performance and consumption of music as a context in which to investigate physical interfaces or physical computing. In this instance, I was interested in de–virtualizing loop–based virtual music, the kind of music often performed on laptop computers. *loopqoob* is an exploration of the areas of 'near instruments', 'plastic playback', and physical computing. It is intended to be a playful and amusing way to play with or perform music. It also aims to be interesting to watch, making the performance of loop-based electronic music observable in a potentially dramatic and physical way, certainly more interesting than watching someone press keys on a laptop. *loopqoob* is a physical performance system consisting of one or more sensor-equipped cubes connected to a computer based music generation/synthesis system. The orientation of the cubes determines an aspect of the music to be played. In this version of *loopqoob*, there are three cubes. Each face of each cube is mapped to a musical motif or loop. The 'cubist' controls which motifs are played by orienting the cubes so that the face corresponding to the desired motif faces up. High intensity LEDs inside the cubes flash in sync with the cube's current motif to assist in determining which cube is doing what'.
– Murat Kumar

Parallel

Loopqoob

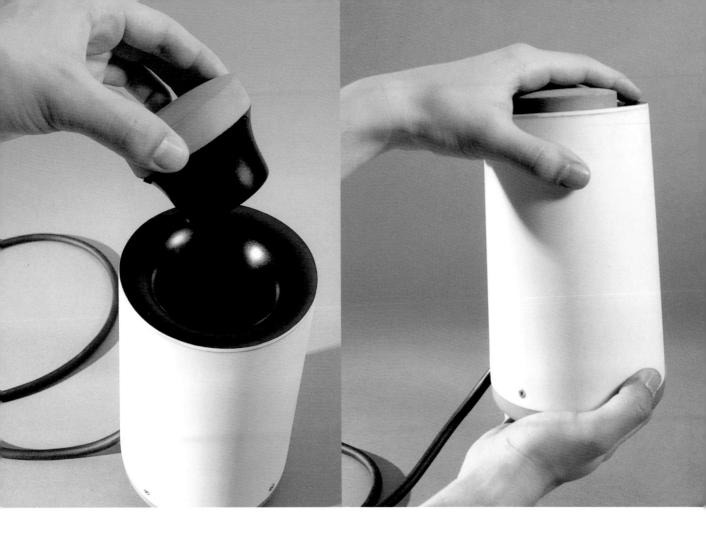

TapTap

KRAM WEISSHAAR

Kram Weisshaar was founded in 2002 as a platform for interdisciplinary research and construction. With offices in Stockholm and Munich, Kram Weishaar works in the areas of industrial design, media design, and architecture.

Clock, Rubber Lamp, Message Board

"The *Clock*, *Rubber Lamp* and *Message Board* are numbers 1–3 of a series of five media products. Each of these projects lives in the space between industrial and interaction design. The *Clock* started out as a screen–based interactive work and eventually began to take three–dimensional form. It seemed a waste to use all of these screen pixels and an expensive display to show something as basic as the time. So we blew up the groups of pixels to much larger than their original size. The new physical pixels are, however, still programmable. By tiling clocks together, one can make a new display controllable from a networked computer. The *Rubber Lamp* addresses a very specific situation that has become an everyday experience for a majority of us: the lighting of the space near a computer. By drawing on the power of the machine itself, we reduce unnecessary cabling and introduce a moment of elegance in an otherwise forgotten space. The lamp is dimmed through the computer itself and a network of lamps can be set dynamically.

"The *Message Board* is a spatial data repository. Messages can be left either over the web, via SMS or directly to the wall using the attached keyboard. With its 64 megabytes of memory, it can hold up to one million messages – effectively becoming a permanent information history for a given location.

"The tools for making industrial productions are actually becoming much more pliant. New machining and production tools can create a million different products one after another, but they are generally used to make the same thing again and again. The limitation is for the most part on the design side – most designers actually don't speak the language of new production. The advantages of these new processes only arise if you use the computer flexibly and interactively throughout the making and production process. We do not use the computer for the sake of using computers or to generate a particular aesthetic – we use it for flexibilty, just to be able to make a room for movement, quality and optimism."

Prada Displays

"The 'epicentre' store concept was coined by the Dutch architect Rem Koolhaas to designate the introduction of new, big stores for Milan fashion house Prada. In 1999, Prada asked Koolhaas's firm OMA to design three stores – in New York, San Francisco and Los Angeles. These stores were conceptualised as 'epicentres' – areas for explosive freedom within the larger, unified whole. "Each of the Prada epicentre stores celebrates the city in one form or another. The Soho epicentre store reflects the diversity, energy, and compression of New York. Digital media as it has been treated in the past largely serves as a force against urbanism. New communication technologies have allowed us to become more and more physically removed from one another. For the Prada epicentre stores, we proposed to reverse this trend. The visitor to the Soho store should be surrounded by a dynamic, vibrant environment enhanced through the use of technology: given better service and more options, but challenged by new ideas about shopping."

Prada Interactive Atlas

"In the most basic sense, the *Prada Interactive Atlas* is a store locator. It helps the visitor to Prada's 'epicentre' store in Soho find other Prada stores. But it also does a good bit more – both functionally as well as conceptually.

"The *Prada Interactive Atlas* serves as a window to an extended Prada presence worldwide. Through the use of the Atlas and other custom media works, the brand makes a preemptive exposure of its own condition. Rather than being threatened by a greater media awareness of its position as a large brand, these works help to explain the conditions and functions of the brand in straightforward, proactive and interactive ways. The interface consists of an overhead projection onto a large table. By moving his/her hand over the table, the user can zoom in and out, examine the position of Prada stores, and re-configure the maps themselves across social and cultural contexts. The design allows for groups of people to share a type of research together and acts as a connection to the other epicentre stores."

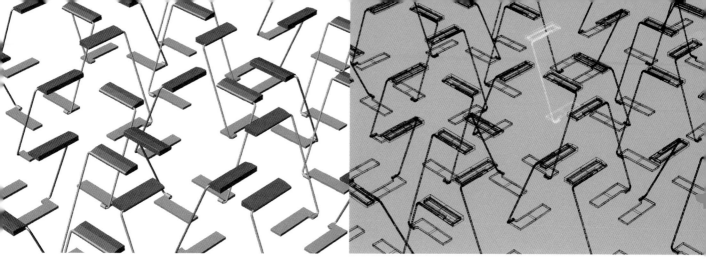

Rubber Lamp

Clock

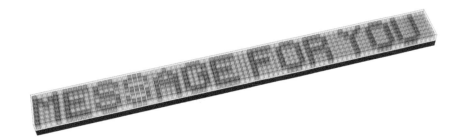

Message board

#120

Prada Displays

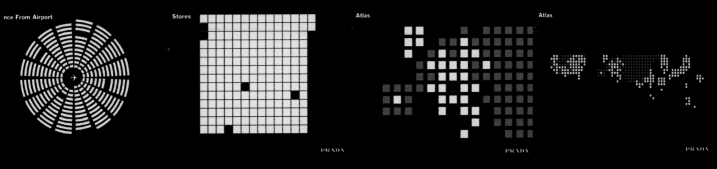

PRADA

PRADA

PRADA

Prada Interactive Atlas

ROMANDSON

"Romandson was founded in 1999 by three members of the antirom collective to provide a more coherent platform for producing projects. Innovation in interactive installations for retail environments and museums continues to form a backbone to romandson's practice."

Composition Station
"The *Composition Station* is made of four flat-touch screens set into a low table in the Science Museum, London. Each touch screen contains one grid. This grid represents a single instrumental part, is monophonic and has a variable number of notes.

"One player controls one grid – via the touch screen. Each player can change their sequence of notes by pressing grid squares. Each player can also control the overall number of notes in their grid, by pressing the plus or minus symbol. Players can combine different patterns and different pattern lengths – say, a pattern of six notes against a pattern of eight notes – to create music in which complexity and beauty emerge from a series of phase relationships. Each player can see the other players' grids and can both see and hear how their sequence relates to the others. The installation is designed to encourage a relationship of mutual cooperation between players.

"*Composition Station* is a development of a software project called *Phase*, which was created at Antirom and used as part of a series of live interactive performances with the string Sextet Instrumental. The project is influenced by, and pays homage to the Indonesian Gamelan, the work of Steve Reich and that of Toshio Iwai."

Andy Allenson adds "With *Phase* I tried to make the simplest visual expression of traditional musical patterns I could imagine. I wanted a system that allowed people to play music and interact with others without any prior knowledge or agreed framework for performance. I found that even with a very restricted choice of notes making a simple musical pattern was sufficiently complex if I added the ability to increase and decrease each pattern's length."

Time and Emotion
"The idea was to create software that would respond to and represent live workplace data from two IBM sites, the first on London's south bank, the second in Hersley, Hampshire, and somehow make visible the labour of the designers and programmers within them. Joe Stephenson explains more: "By monitoring various repetitive activities within the organisation, from keystrokes and mouse movements to movement around the building, it was possible to create an image of the volume and type of activities, and ultimately the emotional state of the building's occupants. The keystroke mountain, for example, creates two heaps of keys based on the number of keystrokes made by occupants of each of the two locations. It creates a playful competition between two remote sites and raises important questions about the relationship of quantity and quality in evaluating work."

Paul Smith
"The brief was to create a physical interactive installation at Paul Smith, London that responded graphically to sound. The Paul Smith sound interactive is a suite of sound toys running on a snow-white Apple iMac, without keyboard or mouse. The only way you can interact with the sound toys is via the built-in microphone input – by shouting or singing. The software comprises eight different interactives based around the character of R. Newbold – a workwear brand owned by Paul Smith. Each toy shows R. Newbold damaging himself in some way or other. For example, in one toy he is holding a hair dryer very close to his head. The hair dryer responds to sound input – the louder the input, the harder the hair dryer blows. If you shout loud enough, the hair dryer blows R. Newbold's head right off. The remaining three toys are abstract representations of sound. They help the user to understand the direct relationship between the ambient sound level in the store and the onscreen visuals."

Red Earth
"Red Earth is a popular make-up brand. Romandson developed attractor software to draw shop visitors to engage with the Red Earth instore kiosk. On approaching the kiosk, the user notices a face on the screen. The face is animating in response to the music and background noise of the store, bringing the image to life by creating an immediate, sensory link between the real-world environment and the screen. Just to see what will happen, the user reaches out a hand – and as their finger touches the screen, the image ripples like a liquid in response."

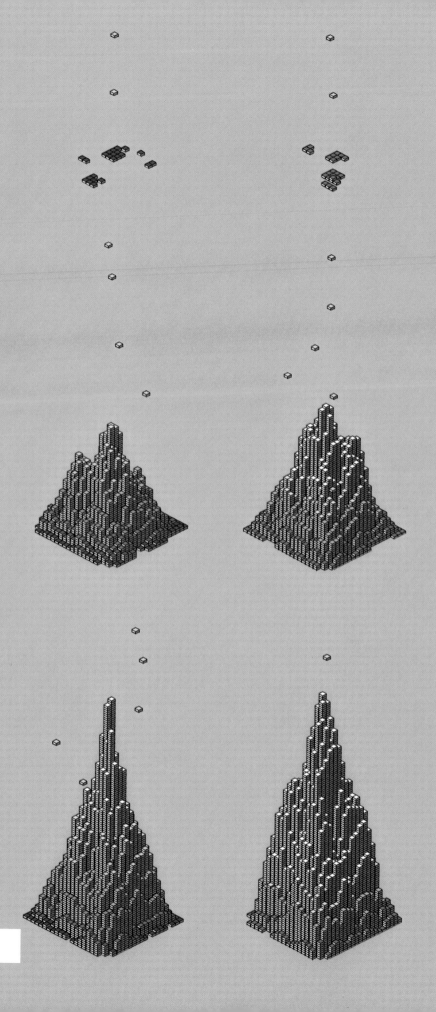

Paul Smith

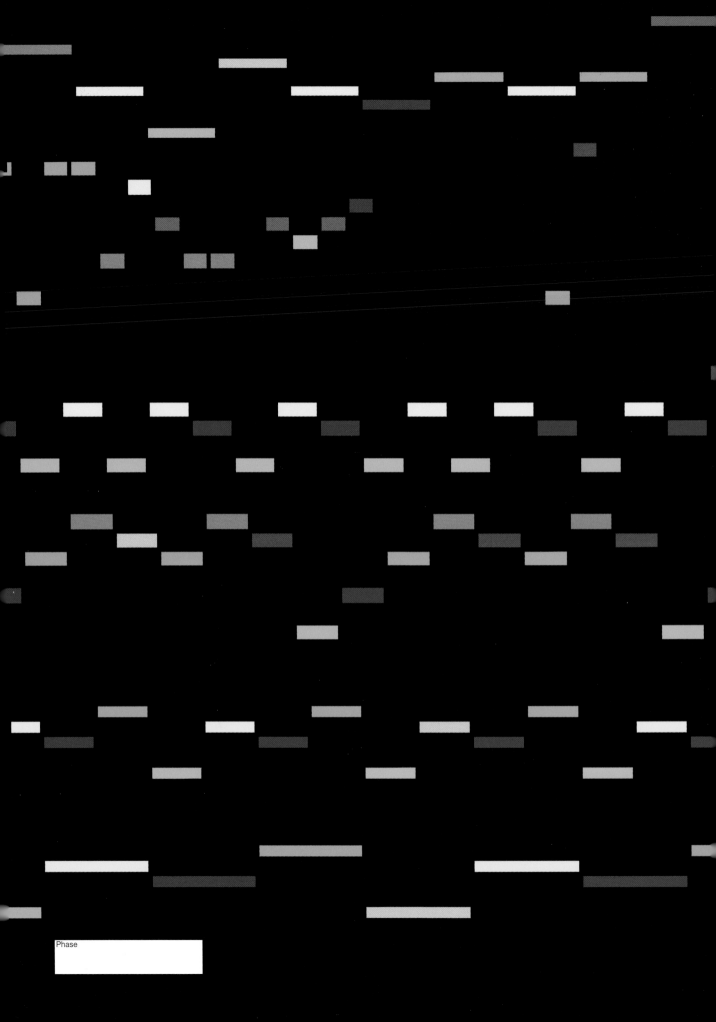

Phase

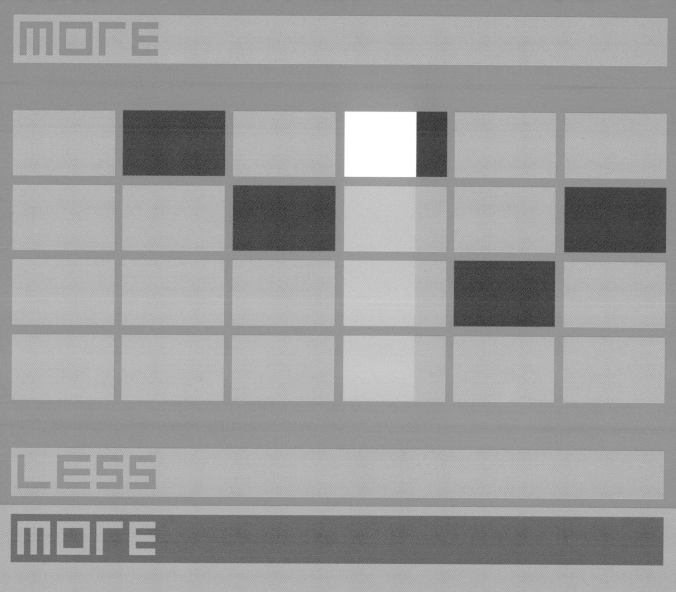

Composition Station

Benetton Jukebox

RYOTA KUWAKUBO

After going to art school, Ryoto Kuwakubo worked as a firmware programmer. There he learned the skills in electronics and programming that led him to become what he calls a 'device artist'. He says: "Many people think that I'm a video-game enthusiast. But I'm not, although I used to play with eight-bit computers up until the end of junior high school. Now I'm working with some toy companies, but it's a shame that I cannot tell you about the project for now! My main creative interest is to create strange situations and make the visitors react against them. I like to make strange devices that people can't help playing with. I try to put funny, serious and ironical things together into a toy-like thing."

Vomoder
"The *Vomoder* is a kind of pseudo videophone. Connect a cable from the headset output of your mobile phone into the terminal on the front panel of the *Vomoder* and call someone. The *Vomoder* will analyse the voice of the person you are calling and change its expression accordingly."

VideoBulb
"Plug the lipstick-like capsule into a video input terminal of a TV monitor to show an animation. It generates a video signal by itself so you don't need any external devices such as a VTR or a computer."

Remakeable T-shirt
"The T-shirts are sold at Muji stores. The prints on the front and the back of the T-shirt are sewing patterns. You can make a stuffed doll by scissoring and sewing along the patterns and stuffing it with soft filling – after you've worn the T-shirt out."

LoopScape
"*Loopscape* is a fighting-game machine for two people using a 360-degree LED matrix display. Each player operates a wireless controller. The rule of the game itself is quite simple: you are in a dogfight and each fighter has to attack the other. Due to the circular nature of the looping display, you have to run around the display following the fighter you control. Moreover, if you fire a missile once then it will fly round and round forever until it hits something. So you might be hit by your own missile!"

HeavenSeed
"The inflatable *HeavenSeed* contains an accelerometer unit at its centre. When you play with it, it produces a sound effect according to the movement you make. For instance, it makes different sounds for throwing, shaking, rolling or spinning."

Duper/Looper
"This is a drum machine with simple interaction. Put it on a table and knock on the table. It will detect the knock through a shock sensor in the bottom, copy it and repeat it. Hold the hammer to stop the drumming."

BlockJam
"A musical sequencer manipulated by physical blocks. It's a research project for breaking the border between players and listeners. Each block represents one beat and one path that a playing point runs along. It has a photo dial with which you can select a sound from pre-set ones. A block with a triangle on the top works as a start/pause button. When you start to play music by pressing the triangle, each connected block triggers a sound step by step."
www.csl.sony.co.jp/IL/projects/blockjam

Bitman
"A tiny, pendant-type electronic display. It has a dance mode in which the character *Bitman* dances, a message mode in which you can show a text you like, an edit mode in which you can edit a text to show, and so on. It also has a tilt sensor so that you can make *Bitman* dance by shaking and rotating the device. The more you shake, the harder *Bitman* dances. It also works as a watch."
www.vector–scan.com

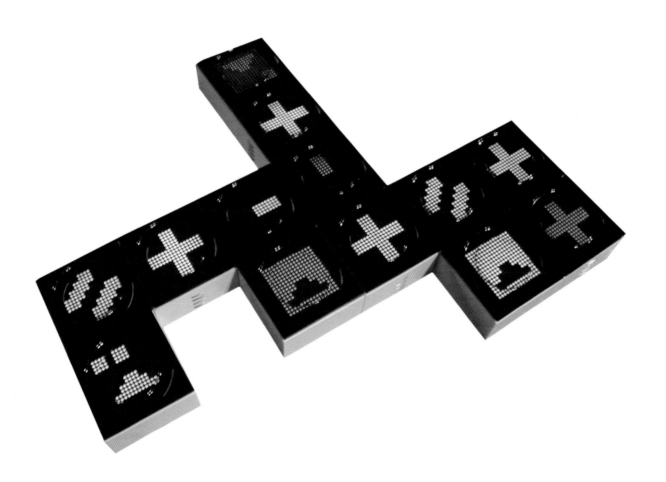

Left to right VideoBulb, Loopscape,
Bitman, Bitman, HeavenSeed,
remakeable T-Shirt

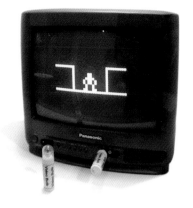

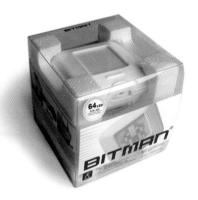

SHOWSTUDIO

Taking Liberties

SHOWStudio was set up by the photographer Nick Knight as a space for personal and experimental work exploring the potential of online and interactive technologies. The Libertys department store fashion project *Taking Liberties* invites passers-by to photograph themselves on the street, using an interactive sensor connected to a camera inside the store window.

Nearly 10,000 anonymous pictures were created by Londoners in March 2004. For Nick Knight, *Taking Liberties* represents a way to engage directly with his audience. "There can be an unhelpful distance between artist and audience," he says. "With SHOWstudio we want to take the gap out, demystify the process, re–establish the direct link with the audience. At the same time, the end product of a piece of work is not necessarily the most interesting part. I wanted a way to show how a piece of work evolves, to share the thrill of making stuff, not knowing how it will come out. The work itself is only the conclusion of a process and sometimes not the most interesting part".

What's it like when the model becomes the photographer, and the photographer loses control over making the picture? "Exhilarating!" he says. "After 25 years in fashion photography, you get to know all the solutions. It's not a nice feeling, so whenever I can I try to lose control, even when I'm in the studio, even on highly commercial projects. It's a bit like standing on the edge of a cliff and throwing yourself off, and desperately trying to clamber back up again. So I am very comfortable with the loss of control inherent in an interactive project. And it's a lot of fun! The creativity and spontaneity come through so strongly. The other day I saw a picture of two women outside Libertys, and it made it seem all worthwhile, just to get those pictures, and for those women to have some fun and make a picture and put it on the Internet. I've always tried to use all kinds of people in my fashion work and this is just an extension of that". Can he see this kind of interactive project becoming more common in fashion? And can he see these images in a fashion magazine?

"Well... I could take it into magazine land, but it doesn't feel right to me. It would be like doing radio on TV, it wouldn't really make sense. It's a fundamentally different medium, with a different structure. There's a desperately exciting new medium out there".

What about as a casting project? "You know, I'd love to be able to get my hands on some of those people, but I can't get hold of them because they don't put their addresses in! The thing is, everyone is interesting. Back in the early days, I'd spend all day photographing someone they told me was beautful, and yet I didn't find them interesting. I'd find the taxi driver who took me home from the studio more beautiful and more interesting than the model. The industry is all about a few people pushing their idea of what is beautiful, you know, the blonde, white, 18-year-old. "If you do a fashion story about, say, older women, or breast cancer, there is an enormous response. People want there to be more diversity, more reality, more honesty. Maybe interactivity can help give control to more people, and things will change…"

Ross Phillips adds "What I like about both *Dare* and *Taking Liberties* is the simplicity with which people can interact and get an instant result. Having said that, I am constantly surprised by what people come up with. Even within the apparent constraints of a single image format, people have created stories, fight sequences, fashion shoots and visual gags. It's as if they want to extend their one shot at self definition into a sequence, creating their own narrative".

suspended"

street fashion shoot

SODA

"Play is central to our philosophy; it fosters an experimental and uninhibited approach to creativity," says a spokesperson for Soda. "Our playing created *Sodaconstructor*, an online construction–kit for building animated models, which won the 2001 Interactive Arts BAFTA Award. *Sodaconstructor* exemplifies our belief in creative play. There are no set goals, instead the users make their own as they experiment and create. It is this flexibility that appeals to our unusually broad audience, encouraging long-term interaction and a great diversity of use. Creative play is rewarding – users discover more as they explore. Their creations are enjoyed and built on by others in turn: a creative snowball effect that sustains the growing Sodaplay community. Play makes our work fun – and generates great content."

2743 and 2743.2

"Eight active, autonomous elements examine the concept of agency within architectural space. These 2 x 1-metre panels flex in continuously evolving patterns controlled by a microprocessor. The software algorithms control the activity of the panels, representing our physical presence and activity in the gallery space."

Corrupted Nature

"Two robots enact de Sade's *Dialogue Between A Priest And A Dying Man,* an argument about the possibilities of free will and the existence of a Creator. This mechatronic tableau ironically questions our views of technology and the artificial within the natural world."

Moovl

"*Moovl* takes the constructionist play pedagogy of *Sodaconstructor* and makes it accessible to a much younger audience by transforming an activity that children already find natural and enjoyable – drawing. It imbues freehand drawings with life-like simulated dynamics and programmable behaviours. This dynamic transformation places drawing in a highly motivating, self-directed feedback process of cause-and-effect, experiment and discovery.

"Developed with *Processing* software, *Moovl* is a work-in-progress premiered at "Design Interactif, Expériences du Sensible" in the Centre Pompidou, Paris, November 19, 2003 – January 5, 2004, and supported by Nesta Futurelab."

ROSE

"Developed by Ed Burton at the Centre for Electronic Arts (Middlesex University), *ROSE* (representation of spatial experience) is a model of young children's drawing behaviour informed by the information-processing metaphor of mind. *ROSE* takes three-dimensional models as its input and produces child-like, two-dimensional drawings as its output. This structure served as the counterpoint for Ed's subsequent research into and development of a new model of children's drawing as a dynamical system: *EOR*."

Corrupted Nature

2743

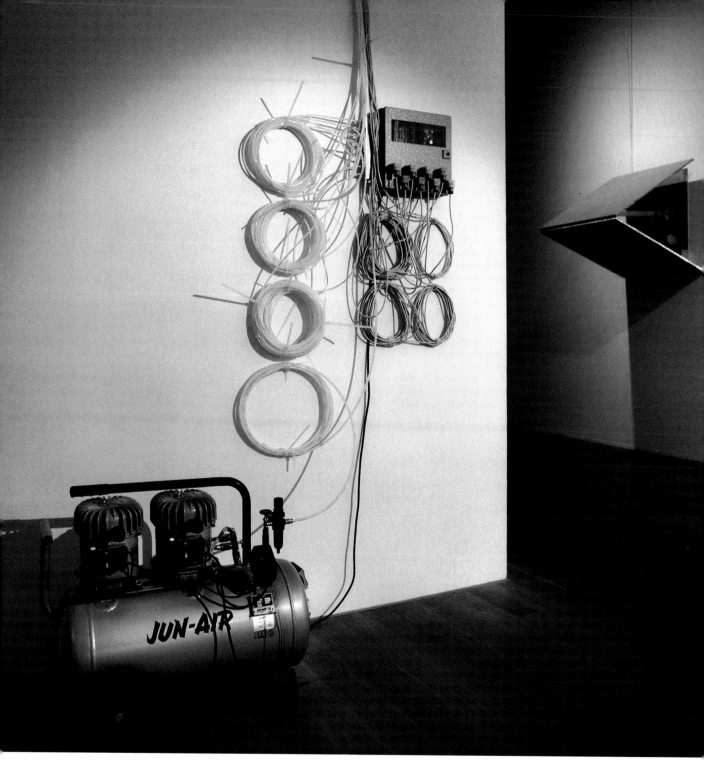

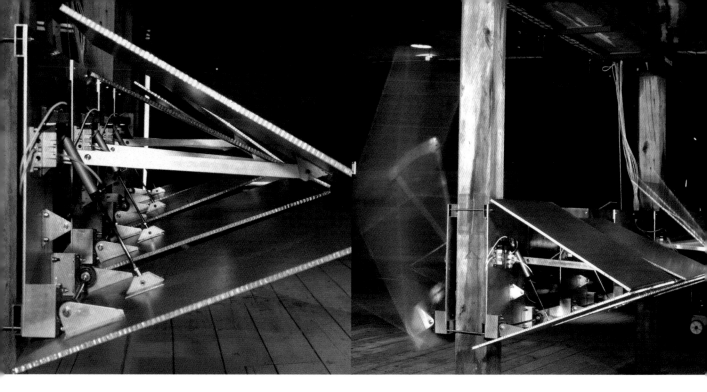

Rose

SUMONA ODENDAAL

Andries Odendaal is an independent Cape Town developer, best known for the work he produced with new media agency Wireframe. His design approach succeeds in being both playful and beautiful at the same time. *Whizzball*, the game he produced for Discovery, is a masterpiece of design and engineering and is a serious contender for the best thing done in Flash, ever.
www.sumona.com

WhizzBall

Whizzball is an online puzzle game developed for Discovery Communications' children's portal. The game explores the concept of 'free play' featuring an open ended environment in which users can construct puzzles for other visitors to the site. Puzzles are constructed by combining various predefined gadgets such as tubes, springboards, catapults and conveyer belts on an isometric play area defined by a 10 x 10 grid. The aim is to construct an obstacle path that can guide a marble from a starting point to an end goal.
http://kids.discovery.com

HP BeetleBuggin

Beetlebuggin is promotional game created for Hewlett-Packard in conjunction with ThincDigital (UK). The game was produced as part of a viral marketing campaign for a European competition, promoting HP products and the new VW Beetle. The game features a miniature sized VW Beetle that is raced around a track built on a desktop featuring various HP products. The aim is to collect all the 'photo paper' that is scattered throughout the isometric environment in the shortest time possible.

C.O.M. e-business

A website commissioned by COM, a German based client. The website features an unusual and playful navigation system. Users navigate through the site by dropping a marble into holes found scattered throughout the isometric terrain.

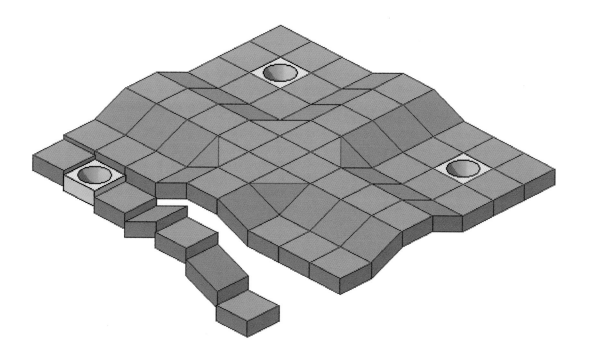

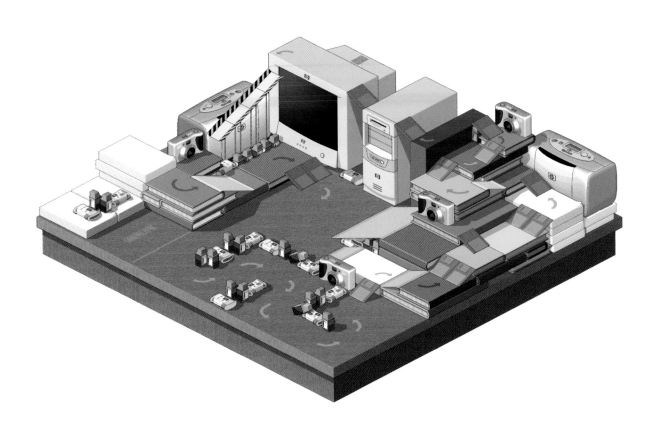

HP BeetleBuggin

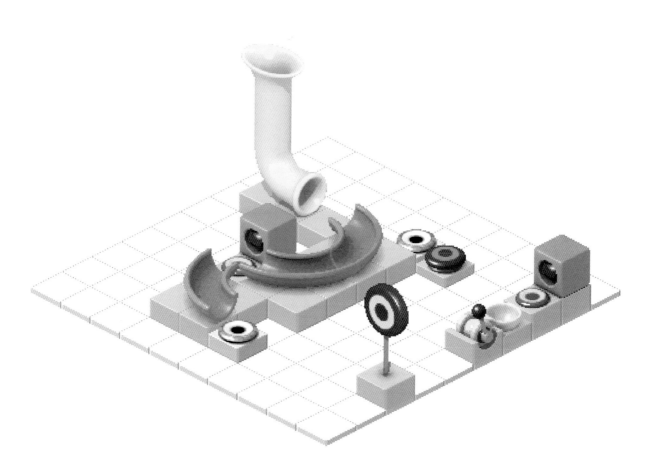

THE INTERACTIVE INSTITUTE SMART STUDIO

Brainball

"*Brainball* is a two-player game where one must be considerably more relaxed than one's opponent to win. The little ball on the game's table is controlled by the player's brainwaves, where both a calm state and a stressed state have a direct influence on the match. The player who is most passive can watch the ball roll away towards the opponent's goal and can be sure of winning. *Brainball* is a game that goes against the conventional competitive concept, and also reinvents the relationship between man and machine. Instead of activity and adrenalin, it is passivity and calmness that mark the truly successful *Brainball* player. *Brainball* is unique amongst machines since it is not controlled by the player's rational and strategic thoughts and decisions. On the contrary, the participants are dependent on the body's own intuitive reactions to the game machine. At first glance, *Brainball* seems similar to a traditional two-player game – two people challenge one and other and take their respective positions at each end of a table that is laid out with two goals and a little ball. The rest of the game's equipment is more special. Both players wear a strap around their forehead that contains electrodes and is wired up to a biosensor system. This system, that is used to measure the body's biological signals, is tightly fastened to the frontal lobes and registers the electrical activity in the brain – a so-called EEG (electro-encephalogram). The players' brain activity is graphed in a diagram on a computer screen so that the public can easily follow the players' mental processes during the match. The brain waves that move the ball forward, increasing the chance of victory, are called alpha and theta waves. They are generated in the brain when one is calm and relaxed. A considerably stressed player will therefore lose. The outcome of the match is rarely obvious since the transition between calm and stress, and vice versa, can occur quickly. Often, the ball will roll backwards and forwards for a few minutes before the game is concluded. In this way, *Brainball* is an exciting and social game where the audience can follow the match by watching the ball on the table, the graph on the screens and the more or less relaxed expressions of the players."

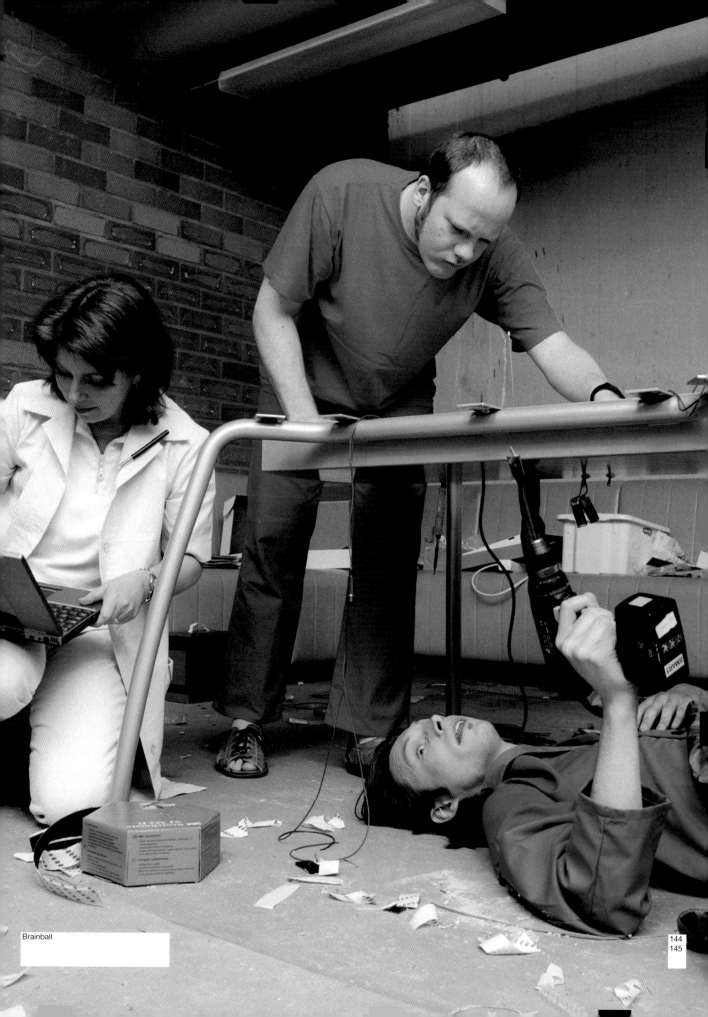

Brainball

Brainball

The Swedish King watching a game of Brainball
between the Västernorrland County Governor
and the Marshal of the Realm

TOMATO

Connected Identity

In 2002, Tomato created an interactive logotype system for Sony. Participants were invited to input a word into the system via an interactive kiosk. The word was then transformed into a 1.5-second 3D animation, and this animation was tacked on to the end of Sony TV spots in Japan. Each advertisement was unique and each contained something unpredictable and unplanned. Michael Horsham explains: "It came out of the notion that the identity shouldn't be fixed, but should be open. It was a philosophical decision – there was a strong interest within Tomato in developing the capacity of the identity to change its behaviour over time. Once this was acknowledged, it became a question of how it could be done. Early on, we spent some time in an edit suite trying out different motions and behaviours and textures and colours. Much of the palette was decided during that process, but then the process of getting it to work in situ created other possibilities and, of course, limitations."

Does interactivity mean the designer loses control? "Design is often a question of orchestrating compromises within an agreed set of parameters – the interesting and exciting bit is often working out what the thing is going to be, so once we'd had the ideas and expressed them into this look and these behaviours, it wasn't a problem. *Connected Identity* is designed to be played with, to change its behaviour in relation to external stimuli, so it was great to see it doing just that. I think that corporate culture is moving away from fixed Paul Rand-style logos. This is a truly interesting cultural phenomenon. It means that somehow behaviours are as legitimate a tool of identity as a fixed sign. The more a behaviour is adopted, the more gestural and fluid an identity can be said to become and arguably, therefore, more human. That's interesting, but whether it's a flash in the pan occasioned by the arrival of affordable technologies or something more permanent, destined for evolution, remains to be seen."

Joel Baumann adds "What is unique about this project is that Sony's customers get to directly affect the brand ID. Whereas corporate communications has in the past all been about top-down control, I think now we will see more projects like this where customers collaborate in the creation of the identity. It's playful and active and it's in line with the way culture and design are developing."
www.sony.co.jp/Fun/ci/

Cube

A cube of water is used as a projection screen for sound volume and image-tracking interactives. The pins of light are reflected by milky impurities in the water and the 2D image is extruded into a luminous 3D block. Users can interact either by making a sound or waving their hands in front of the camera. The milky–water effect is achieved by the addition of a secret ingredient.

Delight in Dedark

Infra-red interactive software development for Ron Arad's *Delight in Dedark*, a translucent silicone rod curtain hung across the gallery space (Ron Arad, Marconi Gallery, 2001). *Delight in Dedark* not only allows you to walk through an image, the image itself also responds to the walkers' movement through the curtain. For example, a virtual sliding door can open for you as you approach the curtain and close, virtually, after you have penetrated the silicone strands, an image can distort around you in ripples, follow you as you walk along the length of the curtain and so on. The movement of people is detected by an array of sensors that send a signal to a computer that manipulates the image. Ron Arad adds: "It was the desire to walk through images that sparked this project, but the space behind the curtain with the spillage of sliced images onto the gallery walls, floor and ceiling was the real delight in the dark."

Wisp

Wisp is an interactive title for PS2 designed by Tomato and featuring work from Tomato and Underworld. Tota Hasegewa explains: "I developed a piece called *Sleeping Eye* with Dirk van Doren, made out of fragments of a movie which Dirk directed. You move the analogue joy stick to reveal the words and links. It's a kind of old school interactivity."

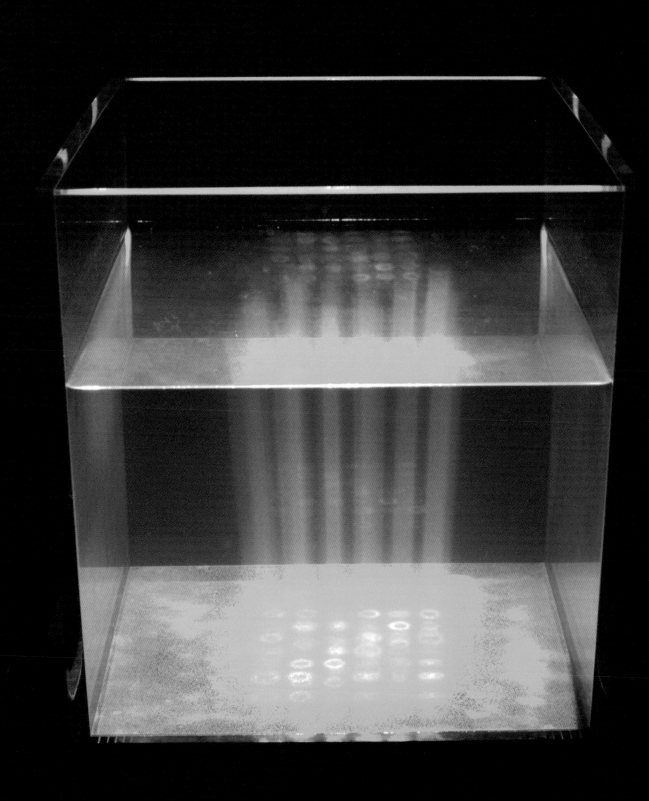

Cube

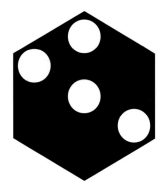

everything leads us to believe

Wisp

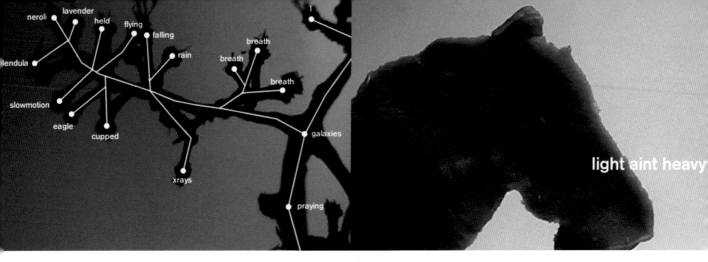

light aint heavy

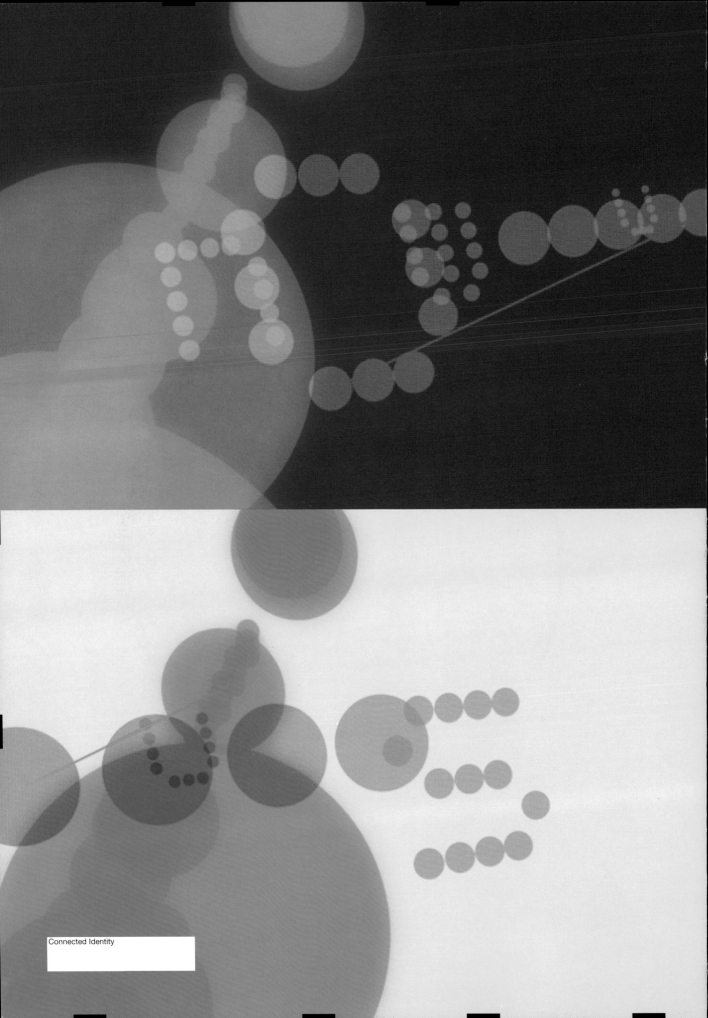

Connected Identity

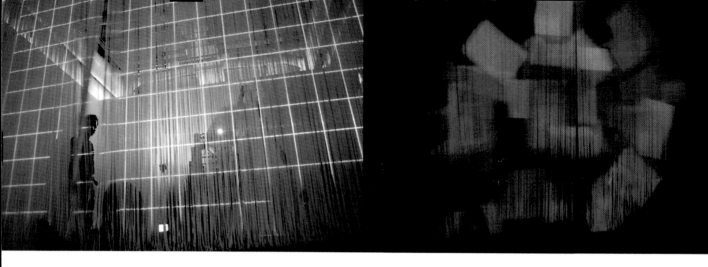

Delight in Dedark

TOSHIO IWAI & KLEIN DYTHAM ARCHITECTURE

ICE – Interactive Communication Experience
Architects Astrid Klein and Mark Dytham invited renowned interactive artist Toshio Iwai to collaborate on an electronic display system for Bloomberg in Tokyo. Together they developed *ICE*, an object they describe as an "icicle", whose function is to collect and precipitate information from a data cloud – rather appropriately for a company such as Bloomberg, which deals in the stuff. *ICE* is actually a large-scale, transparent display case hanging from the ceiling that shows financial data scrolling across its surface. If a visitor approaches the case, sensors will detect a human presence and offer a range of interactive toys and games. *ICE* is an extraordinary collaboration between architecture and interaction design.

156
157

Contributors

Photo Credits

Antenna
Antenna Design New York Inc.
119 West 23rd Street Suite 800
New York, NY 10011 USA
www.antennadesign.com

Antirom
joe@romandson.com
www.antirom.com

Ars Electronica Futurelab
Hauptstr. 2, A–4040 Linz, Austria
T +43 (0) 664 8126239
F +43 (0) 732 7272 680
futurelab.aec.at

ART+COM
Medientechnologie und
Gestaltung AG
Kleiststrasse 23–26
D–10787, Berlin, Germany
www.artcom.de

The BigSpace
via tanaro 10/12
20128, Milan, Italy
www.thebigspace.com

bitforms
529 west 20th New York
New York, NY 10011, USA
T +1 212 366 6939
www.bitforms.com

Boutique Vizique
T +32 477 56 97 23
T +1 415 552 2124
www.boutiquevizique.com

Danny Rozin
www.itp.nyu.edu/danny

Delaware
mail@delaware.gr.jp
www.delaware.gr.jp

Digit
54–55 Hoxton Square
London N1 6PB, UK

T +44 207 684 6769
info@digitlondon.com
www.digitlondon.com

Fabrica
via ferrarezza
Catena di Villorba,
31050 (TV), Italy
andyc@fabrica.it
T +39 0422 516228

Frog
Frog Design inc.
1327 Chesapeake Terrace
Sunnyvale, CA 94089, USA
www.frogdesign.com

Futurefarmers
499 Alabama Street, #114
San Francisco, CA 94110, USA
www.futurefarmers.com
www.antiwargame.org
www.atlasmagazine.com
www.theyrule.net
T/F +1 415 552 2124

Golan Levin and Zach
Lieberman – Tmema
www.tmema.org
www.flong.com

IDEO
White Bear Yard
144a Clerkenwell Road
EC1R 5DF, London, UK
T +44 20 7713 2600
www.ideo.com

Kram Weisshaar
www.kramweisshaar.com

Landesign
Land Design Studio Ltd.
7 Blake Mews, Kew
Richmond-upon-Thames,
Surrey TW9 3QA, UK
T +44(0)20 8332 6699
F +44(0)20 8332 6095
www.landdesignstudio.co.uk

Rafael Lozano–Hemmer
www.lozano–hemmer.com

RCA
www.interaction.rca.ac.uk

Romandson
rom and son, third floor
17–25 cremer street
London E2 8HD, UK
T +44 020 7702 7955
www.romandson.com

Ryota Kuwakubo
www.vector–scan.com

SHOWstudio
Export House
25–31 Ironmonger Row
London EC1V 3QN, UK
T +44 (0)20 7253 4333
www.showstudio.com

SODA
17–25 Cremer Street,
E2 8HD London UK
T +44 [0]20 77396217
F +44 [0]20 77398650
www.soda.co.uk
www.sodaplay.com
www.sodarace.net

Sumona Odendaal
www.sumona.com

The Interactive Institute
Smart Studio
www.smart.tii.se

Tomato
The Tea Building
5–11 Bethnal Green Road
London E1 6LA, UK
T +44 207 033 0455
www.tomato.co.uk

Tohsio Iwai Klein–Dytham
Architecture
www.klein-dytham.com

Every effort has been made
to give accurate copyright
information for photography.
Please contact the publisher
if you have further information
about unaccredited images in
this book.

p. 9–11
Ryuzo Masunaga
p. 12–13
Paul Warchol Photography
p. 14–15
Ryuzo Masunaga
p. 17, 19
Joe Stephenson
p. 21–23
Pascal Maresch ,
Ars Electronica Futurelab
p. 25
ART+COM, Berlin
p. 26–27
R.Horn, ART+COM,
Triad, Berlin
p. 35
Bitforms
p. 35
Casey Reas
p. 37–38
Boutique Vizique
p. 43–49
Israel Museum, Yossi Galanti
p. 56–57
Cat Vinton
p. 61
Wendy Stulberg
p. 62
Evan Kafka
p. 73
Golan Levin
p. 95
Landesign, Nick Wood
p. 122
Sony Corporation and Sony
Computer Science Lab
p. 145–146
Tobias Sjödin
p. 147
Mathias Lindquist, Technicus

International designers Network
IdN Special 04: The art of
Experimental Interaction Design
ISBN 988-97065-8-X

2004 First Edition Published
bimonthly by Systems Design
Limited Shop C, 5-9 Gresson
Street, Wanchai, Hong Kong
T (852) 2528 5744
F (852) 2529 1296
www.idnworld.com

Publisher: Laurence Ng
Editor: Bill Cranfield
Assistant Editor: Chloé Tang
Editorial Assistant: Alva Wong
Senior Designer: Bryan Leung
Marketing Manager: Stephanie Ho
Marketing Executive: Grace Li
Circulation Manager: Flora Kwok
Production Manager: Ngan Kwok Man

Edited and designed at Fabrica
via Ferrarezza, Catena di Villorba
31050 (TV) Italy
T +39 0422 516228
www.fabrica.it

Guest Editor:
Andy Cameron
andyc@fabrica.it
Art Director:
Francesco Menenghini
batterienonincluse@libero.it
Paolo Palma
info@paolopalma.com
Senior Designer:
Mark Taylor
mark.taylor@fabrica.it
Designer:
Vladimir Dubko
vladimir.dubko@fabrica.it
Graphic Artist: Eric Ravelo
erikravelo@hotmail.com
CD-ROM Authoring:
Andy Huntington
Editorial Assistant:
Gabriel Rauter

Subscription:
sub@idnworld.com
General Inquires:
info@idnworld.com
Advertising:
stephanie@idnworld.com
Press releases send to:
press@idnworld.com

Film Output and Scanning:
Commercial Prints
T (852) 2528 5311
F (852) 2529 1296

Printing:
Noble World Printing Co. Ltd
4/F, Shing Dao Ind. Bldg, 232
Aberdeen Main Road, Aberdeen,
Hong Kong
T (852) 2814 1355

Àcumen

Wrapper printed on New-G Gloss
Art Paper 128gsm
Cover printed on Iggesund Creato
Gloss Art Board 350gsm
Text printed on New-G Gloss Art
Paper 150gsm

Submissions:
IdN is pleased to receive
any information on new and
interesting products but is
under no obligation to review
or return unsolicited products
or material. If you would like
to submit an idea for an article,
please send us an outline and
some information about yourself.
Use email if possible.